Leading with Dignity

Leading with Dignity

*How to Create a Culture That Brings Out
the Best in People*

DONNA HICKS, Ph.D.

Yale UNIVERSITY PRESS

New Haven and London

Published with assistance from the Mary Cady Tew Memorial Fund.

Yale University Press books may be purchased in quantity for
educational, business, or promotional use. For information, please
e-mail sales.press@yale.edu (U.S. office) or sales@yaleup.co.uk
(U.K. office).

Set in Minion type by Integrated Publishing Solutions, Grand
Rapids, Michigan.
Printed in the United States of America.

Library of Congress Control Number: 2018932954
ISBN 978-0-300-22963-9 (hardcover : alk. paper)
ISBN 978-0-300-24845-6 (paperback)

A catalogue record for this book is available from the British
Library.

10 9 8 7 6 5

For all the dignity agents out there who know we can do better

Contents

Part III: Creating a Culture of Dignity

Preface

I was in my office one afternoon, working on a project for an organization in Northern Ireland, when the phone rang. I picked it up, and on the other end of the line was a consultant who had been working for a major U.S. corporation for several years. For a minute, I was concerned that he had called the wrong person, but the more he talked, the more I realized he was knowledgeable about my approach to resolving conflict with dignity. At this point, my curiosity was piqued. Why was he calling me?

He explained that the company had been plagued with problems between employees and management for several years, and a senior vice president had given him the task of finding "a unique and creative approach" to resolving conflicts. The consultant told me that he had read online about my dignity work and was wondering whether I would be interested in meeting with him and the senior vice president to discuss longstanding conflicts in the organization. I was initially taken aback, because I had never consulted in the corporate world; for more than two decades, my career had focused on facilitating dialogues for parties in intractable international conflicts. The more I listened to the consultant, however, the more I realized that the issues that were dividing the employees and management of the company were dignity related. Could it be that the approach I had developed for my work in international conflicts around the world was applicable to the corporate environment?

Soon thereafter, I met with the consultant and the senior vice president, and we launched a five-year project with the company. I quickly discovered that conflicts in the business world share many of the same core drivers that are present in international disputes. The common denominator is the human reaction to the way people are being treated. I learned that when people experience violations to their dignity in the workplace, they feel some of the same instinctive reactions that parties in international conflicts experience—a desire for revenge against those who have violated them. People want their grievances listened to, heard, and acknowledged. When this doesn't happen, the original conflicts escalate, which only deepens the divide.

Also similar is the role that leadership plays in these conflicts. Although significant and complex forces always contribute to the breakdown of relationships, the extent to which leaders pay attention to, recognize, and understand the dignity concerns underlying people's grievances makes an enormous difference as to whether these conflicts can be resolved.

As simple as that sounds, it is an enormous challenge, largely because most people do not have a working knowledge of dignity. I have found that most people are unaware of their own inherent value and worth, and are usually at a loss for how to recognize it in others. This ignorance causes a lot of emotional pain and anguish as well as failed relationships of all kinds. Nevertheless, everyone seems to have an instinctive feeling about dignity. We may not have words to describe it, but the truth is, it is deeply embedded within us. What we do know is that *we all want to be treated in ways that show we mat-*

ter, and when we are not treated this way, we suffer. An understanding of dignity—what I call *dignity consciousness*—can take us a long way toward relieving that suffering.

In my first book, *Dignity: Its Essential Role in Resolving Conflict* (Yale University Press, 2011), I showcased the Dignity Model to clarify what dignity is, what it looks like, and how to apply the concept to our lives and relationships. The building blocks of the model are the *ten essential elements of dignity*, which are ten ways to honor dignity, and the *ten temptations to violate dignity*, or ways in which our evolutionary legacy set us up to violate our own dignity. The model also highlights ways to resolve conflict using a dignity approach.

Since the publication of *Dignity*, I have consulted with a variety of organizations interested in addressing relationship problems in the workplace. Their questions and concerns have led me to understand that there is a great need for this vital information in the business community and beyond. *Leading with Dignity* is my answer to this need, and it is designed for leaders in any work environment: in healthcare, education, faith communities, governments, and other organizations.

My goal is to take the dignity work several steps further by showing *dignity in action*. This sequel, then, is meant to be a user's guide for leaders who want to expand not just their understanding of dignity, but also their knowledge of how to embody, model, and make it work for the well-being of their people and organizations.

The rewards of putting dignity into practice in the workplace aren't limited to what happens within the organization. There are ripple effects; we can experience them in every encounter, every day, in big and small ways. Knowledge of dignity transforms into a way of being, because the more we engage dignity's potential, the more we become empowered by it.

Acknowledgments

It has been a joy introducing the Dignity Model to people in organizations of all kinds. I've worked in the corporate environment, healthcare, schools, and faith communities as well as with people who have suffered multiple indignities in international conflicts. The contributions that they have made to the development of my thinking about the transformative role that dignity can play in the exercise of leadership are invaluable to me. All of you dignity agents out there who have committed to practicing dignity as a way of life—thank you, thank you, thank you.

Freelance writer Sharon Hogan, who helped me with *Dignity*, also made a significant contribution to this manuscript. Even though she was juggling many of her own life's challenges, she made time to help with editing and thinking through many aspects of this book. I would also like to acknowledge the pivotal role my former literary agent, Coleen Mohyde, played in preparing my original proposal for Yale University Press.

I cannot thank my editor, Jean Thomson Black, enough for her ongoing support and encouragement during the writing process. I don't know how I got so lucky to have her guide

me twice through the production of my books. Thank you,
Jean. I am most grateful to Julie Carlson for doing such a great
job copyediting the manuscript. Also thanks to Michael De-
neen and Ann-Marie Imbornoni at Yale University Press.

I also want to acknowledge with gratitude those who
read and reread the manuscript—Carolyn and Brian But-
ler, Maria Hadjipavlou, Manuel Guillen, and Tomas Baviera.
Many thanks as well to Michael Pirson and all his colleagues
in the Humanistic Management Network, including Sandra
Waddock and Erica Steckler, who have dedicated themselves
to creating a new business paradigm where human dignity
plays a central role. A big thanks to Hugh O'Doherty and
Tim O'Brien for giving me the opportunity to inject dignity
into their leadership conferences. Thank you to my friends at
the W. Michael Hoffman Center for Business Ethics at Bent-
ley University—Mike Hoffman, Bob McNulty, Mary Chias-
son, and Gail Sands. A big thanks to Anne D'Avenas and the
leadership team at Mt. Auburn Hospital, as well as to Andrew
Modest, Stephanie Page, Rebecca Logiudice, and Patrick Gordon. Thank you Paolo Carozza, Steve Reifenberg, and everyone at the Kellogg Institute for International Studies. To Gary
Krahn and all the amazing dignity educators at La Jolla Country Day School, Trinity Valley School, and Berkeley Carroll
School, a big thank-you. Carol Gramentine, Mike Wilpur, and
Megan Saxelby, you are master dignity educators. Another big
thanks to Davie Floyd for the big contribution you made to the
Dignity Model. Also thanks to Diane Sammer, another dedicated dignity educator. My deepest gratitude to Evelin Lindner
and Linda Hartling for their seminal work on dignity. They
are shining examples of what it looks like to lead with and for
dignity. I would like to also thank my friends at Overland Resource Group. Dave Nichol—I cannot count the contributions

you have made to my thinking about dignity. And a big thanks to Archbishop Desmond Tutu for his ongoing support of my work. I also give thanks and recognition to Cynthia Guyer at Global Dignity.

To my mother, Wanda Hicks, and to Debi Hicks, Brenda Browdy, Susan Muzio Blake, Monica Meehan McNamara, Carrie O'Neil, Herb Kelman, Susan Hackley, Paula Gutlove, Liz Lee Hood, Jeff Seul, William Weisberg, Leonel Narvaez, Camilo Azcarate, Buddy and Gail McDowell, Sherry Streeter, Jon Wilson, Maureen McCall, Ron Gregg, Amanda and Richard Curtin, Geralyn and Rob Grey, and all of my gym buddies at Mt. Auburn Club—you are my home team that supports me on a daily basis.

A special thanks to Maria Nicoletta Gaida, my Ara Pacis dignity partner. The work we have done together creating opportunities for our Syrian and Libyan colleagues to restore their wounded dignity has fortified my belief in the transformative power of dignity.

I would be remiss if I neglected to mention the role that Fresh Pond has played in creating the ideas in this book. Whenever I would get stuck and unable to think straight, my husband, Rick, and I would look at each other and say, "Let's push the refresh button and go for a walk around Fresh Pond." There is nothing like taking a step into the natural world to get clear, get grounded, and to be reminded of the power that resides in our connection to it.

To my husband, Rick Castino, I owe everything. Together we are a living dignity laboratory, continually testing ideas that push the boundaries of our capacity to love and our shared commitment to creating a world with less suffering and a whole lot more fun.

Leading with Dignity

Introduction

The most exciting breakthroughs of the twenty-first century will not occur because of technology, but because of an expanding concept of what it means to be human.

—John Naisbitt

Every time I give a talk about dignity, I always start with a slide featuring this quotation by the futurist John Naisbitt. He has summed up in one line the conclusion that I have come to after more than a decade of research into why a feeling of worth is so important to people. Dignity not only explains an aspect of what it means to be human, but also is a hallmark of our shared humanity. *Everyone wants to be treated in a way that shows they matter.* What does this common desire to be valued tell us about the human experience? Are we too dependent on others for the acknowledgment of our inherent value? How does an awareness of dignity influence our ability to lead people so that they recognize their own value and worth as well as the dignity of others?

Our universal yearning for dignity drives our species and defines us as human beings. It's our highest common denominator, yet we know so little about it. It's hard for people to articulate exactly what it is. What they do know is more like an intuition or a sixth sense. "Yes, dignity is important," people tell me, but they come up short when I ask them to put their intuition into words.

What people usually say is that dignity is respect. I get this response every time I ask an audience. But dignity is not the same as respect. Dignity, I argue, is an attribute that we are born with—*it is our inherent value and worth*. I then show a slide of a beautiful infant and say to the audience, "In case you doubt our inherent value and worth, take a look at this precious child and tell me she doesn't have value and worth." A picture speaks a thousand words—I usually don't have to go any further to convince them. *We were all born worthy.*

Respect is different. Although everyone has dignity, not everyone deserves respect. Respect must be earned. If I say I respect someone, it is because he or she has done something that is extraordinary—gone the extra mile to deserve my admiration. The actions of that person inspire me. I say to myself, "I want to be like that person." Dignity is something we all deserve, no matter what we do. It is the starting point for the way we treat one another. To clear up any confusion, I think it is imperative to respect each other's dignity.

My first book, *Dignity: Its Essential Role in Resolving Conflict,* explored the concept of dignity and gave readers a concrete way of thinking about what it is, why it is important, and what it looks like in everyday life. I introduced the Dignity Model—an approach to resolving conflicts that highlighted our shared human desire to be treated well. For example, in a section entitled "The Ten Elements of Dignity," I introduced concrete ways to honor dignity, such as treating people fairly and accepting their identity no matter their race, religion, ethnicity, or sexual orientation. In another section, "The Ten Temptations to Violate Dignity," I described ways in which our biological hardwiring sets us up to violate our own dignity as well as the dignity of others. For example, the desire to get even and seek revenge is a hardwired response to threat, part of our self-preservation instinct.[1] I then proposed ways to use the concept of dignity to repair broken relationships.

What drove me to write that book was a compelling need to share with the world this fundamental aspect of the human condition that had not been adequately examined. I felt I had uncovered an example of what Naisbitt was writing about: *a truth that expands our concept of what it means to be human.* That truth is the awareness of the vulnerability we all face when someone treats us as if we don't matter. The power behind a violation of our dignity can destroy relationships, breaking the bond of trust that is essential in healthy human connections. And yet when we honor the dignity of others, it creates a sense of safety between us; people feel free to make themselves vulnerable, free to reveal their true selves. Relationships thrive when both parties feel they are seen, heard, and valued.

The greatest insight that comes from knowledge of dignity is the recognition of the internal power that comes along with claiming our inherent value and worth. It helps us to "hold steady" when something bad happens to us, frees us from thinking that our value and worth depend on how others treat us, and enables us to bounce back when our dignity has taken a hit.[2] Knowing that our dignity is in our hands, that we are in charge of it no matter what the circumstances, makes us resilient and able to stay connected to our worthiness.

I learned this from Archbishop Desmond Tutu when I

worked with him in Northern Ireland.[3] It was at a time when I was grappling with the concept of dignity, trying to define it and establish some basic principles about how it works in our lives. I explained to him that so many of the people I have worked with in international conflicts influenced my thinking because they commonly reported that they felt "the other side" had stripped them of their dignity. Their fight was about regaining their lost dignity.

After I said that, he gave me a look I will never forget. He tilted his head, scrunched up his face, and said, "What are you talking about? No one has the power to strip us of our dignity! How do you think we got through apartheid? Knowing that our dignity was in our hands, and in our hands only, sustained us in those darkest moments." He then told me to read Nelson Mandela's book *Long Walk to Freedom* to get Mandela's take on the subject.

The first thing I did when I got back home was to go to the bookstore and buy the book. The part that Archbishop Tutu was referring to was when Mandela described the day he entered the Robben Island prison in South Africa. Mandela decided that one of the first things he had to do was figure out what the guards were up to so that he and his fellow political prisoners could survive. He realized very quickly what the guards were trying to do: *strip them of their dignity.* Here's what he said: "Prison and the authorities conspire to rob each man of his dignity. In and of itself, that assured that I would survive, for any man or institution that tries to rob me of my dignity will lose because I will not part with it at any price or under any pressure."

This insight has become one of the basic building blocks of the Dignity Model. I call it *Mandela consciousness.* One of the major misconceptions about dignity is that we think we gain our sense of worth from external sources. We feel good when we get validation from others in the form of praise, approval, and being recognized for our good deeds. There is nothing bad about enjoying that kind of recognition. What so often happens, however, is that if we don't get the praise and approval that we are so desperately seeking, we feel miserable. If we mistakenly think our dignity comes only from external sources or from the way others treat us, we are giving up a tremendous amount of internal power—power that gives us resilience, enabling us to ward off assaults and stay firmly grounded in the truth of our worthiness.

Every time I get sidetracked from this truth, I think of Archbishop Tutu looking at me with that scrunched-up face as if I had said the stupidest thing in the world. Well, as it turns out, my thinking was not only wrong, but also dangerous. Not being aware of the biggest gift we are given at birth—the invaluable gift of dignity—gets us into such deep trouble. All sorts of morbid symptoms appear when we lose sight of our dignity.

Knowing that we have dignity and that it is always with us allows us to be more vulnerable with others, take risks, and speak the truth. *Vulnerability is where the truth lies.* The more we can be honest and truthful, the less we violate our own and others' dignity, and the more our relationships flourish. When we lose a firm hold on the belief of our inherent value, when we question our own worth, we are more likely to engage in face-saving behaviors that wreak havoc on relationships. I will comment more about these self-defeating behaviors later in the book.

Not being aware of dignity's inherent power also creates a problem for leadership. Elizabeth Samet has a unique take on this power failure. In her remarkable book *Leadership: Essential Writings by Our Greatest Thinkers,* she writes that there is a crisis of leadership because people are looking outside of themselves for the next leader to emerge.[4] "We are waiting to be rescued," she explains. She believes that we all need to become more confident in our ability to lead and points out the danger of looking outside of ourselves for someone to save us. She sums it up with a quotation by John Adams: "There would be little improvement in social and political organization until the people learn to consider themselves as the fountain of power, and until they shall know how to manage it wisely and honestly."

Dignity is a big part of that learning. Regardless if our concern is leading our personal lives or leading an organization, a key to being successful is *dignity consciousness:* a deep connection to our inherent value and worth and to the vulnerability that we all share to having our dignity violated.

If we are to consider ourselves a "fountain of power," we first need to know, intimately and confidently, that it exists within us. Dignity is the source of priceless power—it enables us to develop mutually beneficial connections to others and to create positive change in our relationships.

Managing our power wisely and honestly can happen only if we recognize the value and vulnerability of ourselves and others so that we do not abuse it. Educating ourselves about dignity is the first step. Knowing and accepting what lies within us will free us from a lot of needless suffering and allow us to live our lives fully.

I gave a talk on dignity at Koç University in Istanbul a few years ago. The president of the university, Umran Inan, opened the conference with the usual welcome to everyone, then said something that I have never forgotten. He said that he felt education should be about "liberating the human spirit." At the time, I thought that dignity, too, needed to be liberated, or that maybe it's the same thing. In either case, education definitely plays a big role in igniting the fire inside our students, getting them to embrace their own "fountain of power" and using it honestly and wisely.

What I know now that I didn't know when I published *Dignity* is that this attribute is linked to many other issues. Its reach extends so much further than I had thought, into the inner workings of the human experience. Once again, I feel compelled to share this information, not only to expand our concept of what it means to be human, but also to contribute to an understanding of the leadership challenges we are facing in our work, organizations, and the world—and how dignity can help to address these challenges.

The knowledge we gain from learning about dignity is far more extensive than just information added to our intellectual repertoire. Learning about dignity involves understanding the complex, often conflicted state of our inner worlds and the emotional challenges we face daily. There are lessons to be learned that can help us become better people, spouses, parents, and many kinds of leaders. These lessons can enable us to develop into the best versions of who we are.

The transformation that occurs with a consciousness of dignity helps us gain perspective—it allows us to take a step away from our usual point of view so we can better understand why we do what we do, why we feel the way we feel, and why we think the way we think. It is about more than learning—it is about *developing* ourselves in a way that makes us wiser rather than smarter. The consciousness that it brings enables us to see our blind spots and ways in which we are held back from living life in full extension—expressing all of our talents, fulfilling deep connections with others, and engaging in a life that has meaning and purpose.

Just like respect, trust has to be earned. Without consciousness of dignity, it is more than likely that at some point resentment and distrust will prevail. Trust requires safety, and the one sure way to ensure that people feel safe is to treat them with dignity.

Dignity in the Workplace

My experience applying the Dignity Model in a variety of settings and organizations has given me insight into the extent to which ignorance of dignity affects the work environment. In my research, I have found that one of the most pervasive violations of dignity is that people do not feel safe to speak up when they feel they are not treated well, especially by their managers and supervisors. They are fearful that if they speak up, they will be reprimanded, receive a bad performance review, or even lose their jobs.

One of the necessities of hierarchical organizational structures is the concentration of power in the hands of a few at the top. There is nothing inherently wrong with hierarchies, but if those who are in leadership positions don't understand dignity, power can easily be abused and misused. Robert Fuller's book *Somebodies and Nobodies: Overcoming the Abuse of Rank,* warns us of the dangers that are inherent in ranking human worth.[5] One of the greatest temptations that leaders have to avoid is believing in their superiority. This is where dignity provides a perfect counterbalance, for *we may differ in status, but we are all equal in dignity.*

As Amy Edmundson points out in her book *Teaming: How Organizations Learn, Innovate, and Compete in the Knowledge Economy,* many organizations rely on the traditional, hierarchical way of working and organizing.[6] The top-down, command-and-control approach worked for decades, but the environment it creates inhibits learning and collaboration. It also inhibits a sense of safety—employees are afraid of speaking up when something feels wrong. These complex human dynamics can be easily addressed with an understanding of dignity.

I have often found that leaders of organizations do not have a working knowledge of dignity and the role it plays in our lives and relationships. The leaders with whom I have worked are good people, but before I arrived they generally had little understanding of dignity and were harming their employees' dignity without knowing it. Their lack of awareness of how their actions were negatively affecting others led me to write this book. Good leaders were violating the dignity of others, not because they were afraid to give up control, but because they didn't know what they didn't know. Good people with good intentions can harm others if they are not conscious of dignity.

Leading with dignity demands that we pay close attention to the effects we have on others. Without such knowledge, relationship problems that plague the workplace will continue. Understanding the powerful forces that are unleashed with a violation of dignity (anger, resentment, and the desire for revenge) as well as when dignity is honored (love, loyalty, and the desire to give of oneself freely) will make it easy for leaders to do what is right. When such consciousness is part of a leader's repertoire, not only do people thrive, but the organization thrives right along with them.

Where would one go to learn about dignity? It seems hard to believe that something so fundamental about the human experience—our shared desire to be treated as significant—has failed to be recognized by our educational system as an important part of our social development.

At one point in this book, I describe three private schools that are taking dignity education seriously. But what about adults? Where would someone go to gain knowledge of dignity? My hope is that this book will address that gap in our education, making it clear what dignity is, what it looks like in everyday life, and how we can leverage its power to become the most empowered, compassionate humans we can be. Although this book targets the role that leaders play in creating a culture of dignity in an organization, *everyone is responsible.* We all have a part to play in preserving the health and well-being of the work environment.

This book will expand our concept of what it means to be human by exploring all the ways in which dignity contributes to our personal growth and development as well as our capacity to maintain vibrant relationships. It will show the role that dignity can play in creating workplace and organizational cultures that foster well-being as well as other desired outcomes. When people feel that they are being treated well, are valued, and are connected to something greater than themselves, they thrive.

We need people in leadership positions who not only understand this, but embody it—who lead their lives with dignity. I have chosen *leadership* as the focus of this book because the world is desperate for fresh ideas on how to address some of our greatest challenges. Although good leaders exist, and many books already tell us how to lead, I feel I have uncovered a missing dimension to leadership that only dignity can address, for dignity plays a fundamental role in ethical leadership.[7]

In exploring the many ways in which people want to be treated by their leaders in the workplace, I provide answers to the following questions: *What do I need to do to show people that I care? How do I know if I am treating them with dignity? How do violations of dignity in my own life affect my ability to lead? What will it take to create policies that positively touch the lives of people, bringing out the best in them?* In this book I will not only explain *why* treating others with dignity is essential to good leadership, but I will also show *how* to create a culture of dignity in any organization.

Leading with Dignity is a user's guide to developing the internal resources that are required to lead ourselves and others to an expanded consciousness—of who we are, what we are capable of, and how we can find meaning in our life and work. This book is for parents, educators, corporate leaders, faith leaders—anyone who has influence over human beings who long to be led by someone they can trust.

I
What You Need to Know to Lead with Dignity

Knowledge and human power are synonymous.
—Francis Bacon

1

How to Honor Dignity

Nothing is more powerful than an idea whose time has come.
—*Victor Hugo*

Anyone attempting to exercise leadership would be wise to include in her or his repertoire knowledge of what it takes to honor dignity. As I pointed out earlier, although we are all born with dignity, we are not born knowing how to act in accordance with this truth. Learning how to honor dignity doesn't come naturally; it needs to be learned.

What does it look like to treat people with dignity? This question was at the top of my list when I started the research for my first book, *Dignity*. At the time, most of the literature on this topic came from philosophy, except for the remarkable work of Evelin Lindner and Linda Hartling, both world-renowned experts in research on dignity and humiliation.[1] They started an international network of people interested in these issues, and they hold conferences all over the world to engage people in a conversation about dignity and related matters. Lindner, too, has written extensively on the topic.[2] Building on these ideas, I pursued answers to my questions about how to make dignity concrete for people, that is, how to describe what it looked like to be treated with dignity in everyday life. When it became clear that there were no simple answers to my practical questions, I began to interview hundreds of people from all over the world, asking them to tell me about a time when they felt their dignity had been honored or when it had been violated. From their stories, patterns emerged—themes that were similar regardless of where the people were from. I also found that people came up with more stories about when their dignity had been violated than about when it was honored, and that the patterns emerged more from the commonalities of when people felt marginalized and mistreated. The stories may have been in different contexts, but the felt experiences of having dignity violated were the same.

These patterns led me to come up with what I now call the "ten elements of dignity," and suggestions for using them to honor others' dignity. While I am open to the idea that there may be other elements of dignity, these ten kept emerging in the stories people told.

Acceptance of Identity. Approach people as being neither inferior nor superior to you; give others the freedom to express their authentic selves without fear of being negatively judged; interact without prejudice or bias, accepting that characteristics such as race, religion, gender, class, sexual orientation, age, and disability are at the core of their identities.

Recognition. Validate others for their talents, hard work, thoughtfulness, and help; be generous with praise; give credit to others for their contributions, ideas, and experience.

Acknowledgment. Give people your full attention by listening, hearing, validating, and responding to their concerns and what they have been through.

Inclusion. Make others feel that they belong, at all levels of relationship (family, community, organization, and nation).

Safety. Put people at ease at two levels: physically, so they feel free from the possibility of bodily harm, and psychologically, so they feel free from concern about being shamed or humiliated and free to speak up without retribution.

Fairness. Treat people justly, with equality, and in an even-handed way, according to agreed-on laws and rules.

Independence. Empower people to act on their own behalf so that they feel in control of their lives and experience a sense of hope and possibility.

Understanding. Believe that what others think matters; give them the chance to explain their perspectives and express their points of view; actively listen in order to understand them.

Benefit of the Doubt. Treat people as if they are trustworthy; start with the premise that others have good motives and are acting with integrity.

Accountability. Take responsibility for your actions; apologize if you have violated another person's dignity; make a commitment to change hurtful behaviors.

When I am invited to consult in an organization, after introducing the ten elements of dignity, I interview people and ask them to talk about a time when they felt their dignity had been violated at work. Even before they start to tell their stories, they are quick to let me know that the dignity approach to understanding the dysfunctional dynamics that take place at work perfectly captures their experience. They tell me that when they have a hurtful interaction with someone, they are left with an overwhelming, negative feeling, and it's difficult to figure out exactly what happened. They express that they are grateful to have a way to understand why they feel so bad (their dignity was injured) and a vocabulary with which to talk about it.

The stories have a familiar pattern. For example, when I interviewed a manager at a large company, he told me that there was so much competition among his fellow managers, all of whom reported to the vice president of their division, that he was beginning to dread coming to work. Everyone was looking for recognition and acknowledgment from the "boss," and in so doing, they ended up trying to make themselves look good, often at the expense of the other managers. They would not give each other the benefit of the doubt; when something went wrong, they showed no interest in gaining a deeper understanding of what happened. Instead, they jumped to conclusions about each other's ability to do the job. They would also find subtle ways to be sure that the vice president would find out about the "incompetence" of their colleagues. They would leave each other out of important meetings and never apologize for the exclusion. The dynamics made it difficult for them to be their authentic selves at work. Female managers in the group reported feeling particularly targeted. They often felt that they were passed over for important assignments and committees and that the vice president had "favorites" who, more often than not, were the male managers. They told me that not only did the environment feel toxic, it felt unsafe; "no one knew when they were going to be thrown under the bus."

This story demonstrates why people walk away from a situation at work feeling so violated. Every one of the elements of dignity was involved in this dysfunctional work environment. Let's take them one by one:

Identity: The women in the group felt they were being treated differently, simply because they were women. The managers themselves were violating each other's identity by trying to make others look bad in the eyes of the vice president. No one felt they could be their authentic selves.

Recognition: It appeared that *recognition* did not flow freely from the vice president. Everyone was competing to receive praise from him.

Acknowledgment: The managers failed to *acknowledge* each other for their good work and did not give credit where credit was due.

Inclusion: There was a lack of inclusion; the managers left each other out of important meetings.

Safety: Many of the managers reported that the environment did not feel safe: "We never know when one of us will be thrown under the bus."

Fairness: There was a strong sense that everyone was not treated fairly, especially the women, who felt excluded from being one of the vice president's "favorites."

Independence: The managers did not feel a sense of control over their lives in the toxic environment. They felt that they couldn't be their authentic selves; instead, the forces acting on them to outperform each other made one male manager feel hopeless about his ability to change the dysfunctional dynamics.

Understanding: Because of the competitive environment among the managers, when something went wrong, people were quick to jump to conclusions about what happened, negatively judging each other rather than trying to gain a greater understanding of what happened.

Benefit of the doubt: No one gave each other the benefit of the doubt. Instead, they were waiting for each other to make a mistake so that they could "look better" in the eyes of their boss. Their default reaction was to rush to judgment.

Accountability: No one apologized or took responsibility for his or her hurtful behavior. It was part of the culture to fail to take responsibility, and everyone resisted confrontation, pretending that nothing hurtful had ever happened. Everyone just kept on with "business as usual."

In another interview, a woman explained to me that she always felt uncomfortable in staff meetings because she never knew who was going to be "called out" in front of everyone. Her boss (we'll call him Tom) often used the meetings to point out those whom he called the "weak links" in the group—people he thought were not working at peak performance. She explained that the work itself is very satisfying and pays well, so she is reluctant to "speak up" to Tom. She doesn't want to lose her job. She said that her fellow employees were frequently fearful of being targeted with Tom's humiliating and public comments.

In this case, the elements involved were safety (everyone feared Tom's humiliating comments); identity (people were being singled out for bad performance); acknowledgment (Tom did not acknowledge the harm he had done); fairness (people felt it was unfair to be targeted publicly); independence (people felt that there was nothing they could do about Tom's humiliating behavior); benefit of the doubt (Tom failed to meet with people privately to see whether his assessment of their performance was accurate—instead, he jumped to conclusions without giving them a chance to explain themselves); and accountability (Tom never apologized for his humiliating behavior).

Why were all these people so unhappy? The stories all describe situations in which people have not been treated well. Some felt that it was unsafe to speak up, others felt they were being treated unfairly, and many felt that they were being discriminated against because of some aspect of their identity that they could do nothing about. The women, for example, felt that the male managers were getting the "glamorous" assignments and they were being passed over. One employee told me: "Tolerating not being treated well at work is part of my job description."

I hear similar stories every time I am called in by an organization to address employee problems. There is nothing unique about them. People everywhere hate being treated as if they don't matter. When I frame their problems as "dignity violations," they are relieved to hear that their reaction to being treated badly is a common problem—*we all yearn to be treated with dignity.*

If we all yearn to be treated with dignity, what does that say about what it means to be human? Matthew Lieberman, a social neuroscientist and author of *Social: Why Our Brains Are Wired to Connect,* explains that being human means we are driven by deep motivations to stay connected with others. *We are wired to be social.* For our early ancestors, from whom we have inherited these motivations, one's survival depended on healthy, collaborative social relations. There is safety in numbers.

Likewise, evolutionary psychologist Robin Dunbar tells us that for our early ancestors, being together in a group was the best defense against being attacked by predators. When predators appeared, our ancestors were much safer in groups than alone. They felt a pleasant sense of safety when they were connected and fear and anxiety when they were not. The more bonded the group, the greater likelihood of collectively warding off dangers of all kinds.

We have evolved with the powerful need to be in relationship with others and the intense longing to be liked and loved that goes along with it. The default setting of our brains wants us to be engaged in thinking about others.[3] Yuval Noah Harari tells us that evolution favored those capable of forming strong social ties.[4] If good social relations have ensured our survival, is it any wonder that threats to our relationships—such as being treated badly by others—make us feel like our lives are on the line? Being disconnected is a painful, life-threatening experience, as Linda Hartling and Evelin Lindner explain in their article "Healing Humiliation: From Reaction to Creative Action." In the article, they describe Jean Baker Miller's notion of the pain associated with "condemned isolation," where people feel locked out of the possibility of human connection.[5]

According to Lieberman, because our brains have evolved to seek connections with others, when relationships break down, it causes great distress. When people experience disconnection or rejection, the pain they feel—he calls it *social pain*—is as real as physical pain.[6] In fact, he explains that social pain and physical pain share the same neural pathways in the brain. This research reinforces stories I have heard over and over about the negative feelings that people report after a bad interaction with their colleagues. These reactions were not "all in their heads." They didn't imagine those painful feelings—they were real.

The wounds that we inflict on one another during a breakdown of a relationship are not only painful, but also often humiliating. Whoever said "Sticks and stones will break my bones, but words will never hurt me" got it wrong. Words can be used as weapons to psychologically annihilate people's dignity—their sense of value and worth. It's like aiming for the heart when you want to physically destroy someone. Words that take aim at dignity can inflict pain that is devastating. But unlike a physical injury, there are no broken bones, no blood, no obvious sign of a wound. The pain that results from interactions that violate dignity remain invisible, causing people to suffer silently.

These verbal weapons can create a disconnect between people even when they are used without awareness of the harm they're causing. Let's go back to the earlier story about the woman whose boss (Tom) publicly humiliated his direct reports in staff meetings. As it turned out, when I interviewed Tom, I learned that he had no idea he was humiliating his staff. In fact, he thought he was motivating them. It seems hard to imagine, but a lot of the disconnections that happen between people are not consciously motivated. Tom had no idea that he was perpetrating violations of dignity with his staff. It is remarkable what leaders fail to notice when they are not attuned to dignity issues. In *The Power of Noticing*, Max Bazerman makes the point that leaders very often miss information that is right in front of them.[7] Tom was quick to learn that there are much better ways to motivate people than by humiliating them in front of others.

This is why knowledge of dignity, a fundamental aspect of what it means to be human, is so important. The emotional volatility associated with having our dignity honored or violated cannot be overstated. When people feel that their value and worth are recognized in their relationships, they experience a sense of well-being that enables them to grow and flourish. If, in contrast, their dignity is routinely injured, relationships are experienced as a source of pain and suffering. For better or for worse, Lieberman reminds us that we will spend our entire lives motivated by social connection.

Another neuroscientist, Bruce Perry, and his co-author, Maia Szalavitz, go a step further and claim that we are "born for love" (the title of their book). They explain that a vast literature shows that the more loving we are, the healthier and happier we are.[8]

Even though our brains are wired with a deep desire for connection, we aren't necessarily wired to know how to sustain it. Honoring the dignity of those with whom we are in relationship is the glue that binds people together. It's the way to make people feel safe, valued, and loved. If that's the case, wouldn't it be wise for all of us to learn how to get better at loving? The ten elements of dignity can show us the way. Honoring dignity is love in action. Human connections flourish when dignity is the medium of exchange.

Why is this knowledge important for leadership? *If we're going to lead people, we'd better understand them.* At the core of understanding the human experience is recognizing the role that dignity plays in our personal well-being and the well-being of our relationships. If our brains' default setting motivates us to seek safety through connections with our fellow human beings, why not take advantage of that knowledge and use it to leverage its potential power? Knowing that people feel most secure when their relationships are intact, and that the strength of those relationships is dependent on the extent to which people feel their worth is valued and recognized, then why not do whatever we can do to create the kind of culture where honoring dignity is a priority? Leaders who understand the power of treating people well will see their people thrive, and they will thrive right along with them. Because when we honor others' dignity, we strengthen our own.

Business scholars are now also recognizing the importance of honoring dignity in the workplace. In Professor Michael Pirson's extraordinary book *Humanistic Management: Protecting Dignity and Promoting Well-Being,* he describes extensive work that is being done by the Humanistic Management Network, a group of scholars from all over the world who are interested in developing a new paradigm for business and management.[9] Challenging the traditional dominant narrative that focuses on self-interest, ruthless competition, and profit maximization, these scholars propose that concern for human dignity be the centerpiece of a new model that extends to the dignity of the environment, and so includes concern for its exploitation. The Humanistic Management Network is committed to the following principles: that unconditional respect for human dignity is the foundation for human interaction; that ethical reflection must form an integrated part of all business decisions; and that seeking normative legitimacy for corporate activities allows for the aligning of good intentions with activities that have the potential to produce good outcomes. Taken together, these three commitments promote human flourishing through economic activities that are life-conducive and add value to society at large. Submitting business decisions to these three guiding principles is at the core of the new paradigm.[10]

Pirson points out that the old business paradigm is based on the notion that what motivate human beings are money and power—that people are greedy and self-interested. The goal of the old paradigm is maximization of wealth and shareholder profit. Pirson challenges that assumption about what it means to be human and instead proposes that we are motivated to be connected with others, that we humans care for others, and that we have a deep motivation to promote the common good.

The centerpiece of the work of the Humanistic Management Network is to showcase the importance of dignity in business and to create business environments where well-being, rather than wealth, is promoted. He provides examples of companies that have embraced the new narrative and are flourishing, right alongside their people.

The *Harvard Business Review* has published several articles about dignity in the workplace and the need to educate ourselves about what it means and how it affects the well-being of employees. Researcher Sunnie Giles conducted a study involving nearly two hundred leaders in more than thirty global organizations in fifteen countries.[11] She wanted to know what people felt were the top competencies of a leader. At the top of the list was demonstration of high ethical and moral standards. She went on to describe what those standards look like. First was the creation of a *safe and trusting environment*—that is, leaders with high ethical standards convey a commitment to fairness, safety, and inclusion, which are all elements of dignity. She also describes the importance of giving employees clear direction while allowing them to organize their own time and work—giving them a sense of autonomy and independence—as well as the fostering of a sense of belonging and connection, both of which are aspects of dignity. Clearly understanding how to honor dignity is one of the core capabilities that people who exercise leadership need in order to navigate through the complex human dynamics in the workplace.

Monique Valcour, a management academic and consultant, describes a common theme in reports from her students: "Leaders who undermine employee autonomy are corrosive because they undermine the dignity of work."[12] She warns that this is a very serious matter because "dignity is fundamental to well-being and to human and organizational thriving." She writes: "The enlightened leader knows how to treat people with dignity."

Sociologist Randy Hodson's comprehensive analysis of dignity in the workplace points in the same direction.[13] Managers who treat people with dignity—who give them a sense of autonomy and independence to work in the way that best suits them, create an open and trusting environment where employees are acknowledged and recognized for their good work, and treat them in a way than enhances their self-worth and the worth of others—are those who succeed as leaders.

Christine Porath, author of *Mastering Civility*, reports that in her extensive surveys, demonstrations of civility (which overlap with the elements of dignity) are associated with being an effective leader.[14] She found that "demonstrating respect" was the most important leadership quality for getting employees engaged and committed in their work.

My experience working with people in leadership positions is that most of them have not been educated about dignity. Valcour also points out that few managers receive any guidance on how to treat people with dignity. With the proliferation of interest in the subject, perhaps we will see more attention paid to learning how to add this invaluable knowledge to leadership education. As Victor Hugo said, "Nothing is more powerful than an idea whose time has come." Dignity's time is now.

2

How to Avoid Violating Dignity

We need to understand ourselves in both evolutionary and psychological terms in order to plan a more rational, catastrophe-proof future.

—E. O. Wilson

Some time ago, I was invited to speak at an executive team meeting of an organization that was considering hiring me to conduct dignity leadership training, with the broad goal of creating a culture of dignity throughout the company. I started by introducing the ten elements of dignity, after which many of the people looked at each other and said, "We're really good at all of this. Honoring dignity is even in our mission statement." I congratulated them and proceeded to introduce the ten temptations to violate dignity—ways in which we are set up to violate our own dignity. It didn't take long for one person to speak up and say, "This is the work we need to do." No one said a word. Everyone kept looking at the ten temptations handout I had given them. After several minutes, the person who had invited me looked at me and smiled. She thanked me for coming and told me she would be in touch. Later that day, she called and said that the executive team had given her a green light to do the dignity leadership training.

This chapter is a review of the ten temptations to violate dignity—our own dignity as well as the dignity of others. It focuses on what you need to know about our shared human experience—insights from evolutionary biology and psychology that shape the way we as humans instinctively react under circumstances of threat, often violating dignity in the process.

After more than a decade of consulting with organizations about using the Dignity Model, I have learned that lack of self-knowledge—not of our individual, unique qualities, but of a broader dimension to self-understanding—is our greatest collective ignorance. That broader dimension is that *we are, first and foremost, defined by being a member of the human species.* At the biological level, we all have common attributes that make us human, setting us apart from other species. As Leonard Mlodinow puts it, "we have an unconscious mind, and superimposed on it, a conscious brain."[1] Unfortunately, these aspects of our shared humanity are not well understood or recognized.

Any evolutionary biologist or psychologist will tell you that we do not come into the world as a blank slate; instead our brains have a complex inherited architecture that predisposes us to act in certain ways, especially under threat.[2] Evolution has given us sensitivities to being violated. These survival instincts can be called up in a matter of seconds when we perceive someone or something that might cause us harm.

Although most of us know that we are hardwired to fight, flee, or freeze when we confront a threatening situation, what we don't know, as E. O. Wilson points out, is that many

other "inherited mental regularities" are part of our evolutionary legacy.[3] Our mental environment has evolved to set us
up for actions and reactions that promote our survival. These
self-preservation instincts are very powerful. If we don't know
that they exist within us, or if we choose to ignore them, we
run the risk of letting them control us before we can control
them. The problem with these instincts is that although they
may act in the service of self-preservation, they have the capacity to wreak havoc on our connections with others.

But the good news is that we are much more than our
hardwired instincts: we have what it takes to mediate these
forces within us. Educating ourselves about the reality of the
traps that evolution has set for us helps us to navigate around
these survival impulses. As Jerome Barkow warns, "Biology is
not destiny unless we ignore it."[4] Knowledge of these mental
mechanisms that predispose us to violate our own dignity can
put us in charge of them.

Whenever we go up against our biology, it feels hard. The
emotional turbulence our survival instincts cause makes it difficult to control them. Choosing to fight them instead of succumbing to them isn't easy. Along with a big dose of restraint
and assertiveness, we can learn to temper the impulse to avoid
looking bad in the eyes of others, to preserve our relationships
instead of a self that is in desperate need of change. We can increase our capacity to manage these emotional reactions, but
it will require awareness that they exist, and a willingness to
work at it.

On the basis of these insights from evolutionary biology,
I have developed the "ten temptations to violate dignity," that
is, ten ways in which our evolutionary legacy sets us up to violate our own dignity and the dignity of others (along with
strategies for outsmarting those impulses):

Taking the Bait. Don't let the bad behavior of others determine your own behavior. Restraint is the better part of dignity. Don't justify returning the harm when someone has harmed you. Do not do unto others as they do unto you.

Saving Face. Don't lie, cover up, or deceive yourself—tell the truth about what you have done.

Shirking Responsibility. When you have violated the dignity of others, admit that you have made a mistake and apologize for hurting them.

Depending on False Dignity. Beware of the desire for external recognition of your dignity in the form of approval and praise. If we depend only on others for validation of our worth, we are seeking false dignity. Our dignity also comes from within.

Maintaining False Security. Don't let your need for connection compromise your dignity. If we remain in a relationship in which our dignity is routinely violated, our need for connection has outweighed our need to maintain our own dignity.

Avoiding Confrontation. Don't allow someone to violate your dignity without saying something. Stand up for yourself. Don't avoid confrontation. A violation is a signal that there is something in the relationship that needs to change.

Assuming Innocent Victimhood. Don't assume you are an innocent victim in a troubled relationship. Open yourself to the idea that you might be contributing to the problem. You may not be aware of it. We need to be able to look at ourselves from an outside perspective so that we can see ourselves as others see us.

Resisting Feedback. Don't resist feedback from others. We often don't know what we don't know. We all have blind spots (undignified ways in which we unconsciously behave). We need to overcome our self-protective instincts that lead us to resist constructive criticism and instead consider feedback as a growth opportunity.

Blaming and Shaming Others. Don't blame and shame others in order to deflect your guilt. Control the urge to defend yourself by trying to make others look bad.

Gossiping and Promoting False Intimacy. Beware of the tendency to connect with others by gossiping about someone else. Being critical and judgmental about others when they are not present can feel like a bonding experience and makes for engaging conversation, but it is harmful and undignified. If you want to create intimacy with others, speak the truth about yourself—about what is really happening in your inner world—and invite the other person to do the same.

The desire not to look bad in the eyes of others, especially those with power and status, has survival value.[5] Threats to one's good standing often trigger these self-preservation instincts. My favorite example of a well-known person who fell into the temptations trap is Lance Armstrong. Although many prominent leaders in business and politics have been equally lured, Armstrong's case is particularly illustrative because he fell for nearly all of the ten temptations by covering up the truth about his use of performance-enhancing drugs. He was so afraid of looking bad in the eyes of the world that he focused on self-preservation instead of on telling the truth. As Jonathan Haidt points out, people are more motivated to protect their reputations than to ensure that the truth becomes known. He says that we are more interested in looking good than being good.[6]

After Armstrong won seven consecutive Tour de France bicycle races, allegations of doping surfaced, instigating an investigation into his drug use. For several years, he claimed innocence; he even fought back by filing a federal lawsuit to halt the doping case against him. The lawsuit was dismissed, and Armstrong began the humiliating process of coming to terms with his public exposure. In the end, he was stripped of all his Tour de France titles and his Olympic bronze medal. None of his corporate sponsors renewed their contracts with him. Not only did he lose his status and power; he also damaged his dignity.

Let's look at the temptations that he could not resist:

Taking the Bait: Armstrong fought back and returned the harm to others in an effort to deflect his guilt. He filed a lawsuit in an attempt to have the charges removed.

Saving Face: Instead of coming clean, admitting that he had used performance-enhancing drugs, Armstrong tried to cover up the truth and engaged in all kinds of deception, including self-deception. After investigating his case, I became convinced that he deceived himself so fully that he came to believe he hadn't used the drugs.

Shirking Responsibility: He lied to others and the world and failed to take responsibility for his actions.

Depending on False Dignity: His desire for external recognition overcame his desire to protect his inherent dignity.

Claiming Innocent Victimhood: He tried to make the world believe that he was being unfairly treated—that he did not violate any rules of the game—and that he was innocent of any charges.

Resisting Feedback: Even when the allegations of his drug use came out, he still denied it, failing to take the feedback as evidence of his wrongdoing.

Blaming and Shaming: Instead of owning up to his bad behavior, Armstrong filed a lawsuit to stop the case against him, claiming others had lied about his drug use.

The fall from grace for someone who is held in such esteem by the world as Armstrong was (both for beating cancer and for winning so many Tour de France races) was particularly reprehensible. The world felt betrayed, to say the least, and the disgust that was felt by so many must have affected him deeply. The shame that he was trying to avoid in the beginning eventually caught up with him. What made him think he could get away with it?

I have often thought that if Armstrong had admitted to using drugs when the allegations first surfaced, the public might have been a little gentler on him. After all, he had survived cancer and people were feeling a lot of empathy for him. But as dignity experts Linda Hartling and Evelin Lindner have suggested, the fear of humiliation runs very deep in us.[7] It appeared that the need to ward off negative public exposure was stronger than Armstrong's desire to protect his own dignity.

Understanding these preprogrammed vicissitudes of our inner worlds might not make decision-making all that much easier when we are lured by the temptations, but we would be aware of the cost of succumbing to them. We would also go a little easier on ourselves when we feel the pull of them, knowing that this is a struggle that we are all up against. The truth is, inner conflict is one of the hallmarks of being human. As Wilson explains, internal conflict is not a personal irregularity but a timeless human quality.[8] The forces that pull us in the direction of self-preservation are always up against our need to be connected with others and to be a part of a group. As we saw earlier, we are social beings who have found safety in numbers, and when we look bad in the eyes of others, we run the risk of being disconnected from them. The shame that is felt when we are exposed for a wrongdoing is so strong that we will avoid it at all costs.

The inner tension that is triggered when we are caught in these powerful competing forces creates turmoil for us. Wilson writes, "Relentless ambivalence and ambiguity are the fruits of the strange primal inheritance that rules the human mind."[9]

If we are aware of this fundamental aspect of our shared humanity, not only might we go a little easier on ourselves, but we could also extend that compassion to others. Instead of crucifying them when they are lured by the temptations, we could hold off on passing judgment and say to ourselves: "There but for the grace of God go I."

Another aspect of the Dignity Model that clarifies what happens to us when we are caught in these instincts to preserve our image, no matter the cost, is the distinction between what I call the "I" and the "Me"—two parts of the self that the philosopher William James first articulated in the nineteenth century.[10] I have adapted his ideas to help explain the tension we often feel when we are lured by the ten temptations.

The "I" is the continuous part of who we are, the part that can overlook the "Me" that is in constant engagement with the world. Think about the "I" as having the ability to take a bird's-eye view of yourself in interaction with the world. The "Me," by contrast, is constantly acting and reacting to what is happening between you and others and reacts instinctively when you experience a violation to your dignity. It is lured by the temptation to preserve the self, no matter what. The "Me" is the part of the self that can function outside of our awareness. Driven by our evolutionary legacy, it wants to look good in the eyes of others, no matter what. It seeks external validation of its worth, constantly looking for praise and approval to feel good. It is vulnerable to criticism and reacts strongly when dignity is violated. This part of ourselves is overly concerned about the judgment of others: the content of its inner dialogue is always about "Am I good enough, smart enough, loveable enough? How do I measure up to others?" This judgment also extends to others. "Am I inferior or superior to them?" Evaluating oneself against others is a preoccupation.

The "Me" is also vulnerable to getting into conflict with others. It is defensive, reactive, and wants only to eliminate the source of the threat. It takes the bait, wanting to get even and seek revenge. The "Me" is the active player in the ten temptations. It will do whatever it takes—lie, deceive, cover up, shirk responsibility—to avoid losing status and good standing with others. It wants to protect the self at all costs.

The "I" is not dependent on others for its sense of worth. The "I" knows that its worth is unconditional. It has Mandela consciousness. It does not need external validation of its dignity. It views feedback as a growth opportunity, not as criticism. It is open to learning especially about aspects of the self that it cannot see but others can.

When we are firmly grounded in the "I," we can experience all dimensions of dignity: a connection to our own dignity, to the dignity of others, to the natural world, and to something greater than ourselves. Unlike the "Me," its goal is self-expansion and growth, not self-preservation.

An objective in dignity work is for us to be aware of both aspects of who we are. If we learn to recognize when we are

"Me" driven, we will be able to fight the impulses that lure us into violating our own dignity—by wanting to cover up our bad behavior because we are fearful of looking bad. We need to develop a relationship between the two parts so that the "I" can come to the rescue of the "Me" when it wants to engage in self-destructive, self-violating behaviors. The "I" has what it takes to overpower the tyranny of the "Me." Instead of looking outside of itself for validation and comfort, the "Me" turns inward, finding refuge in the "I."

Knowing this about ourselves—that we have the internal resources to hold ourselves back when we feel the lure of the temptations—puts the power back into our hands. We do not have to be a slave to our instincts. We have what it takes to choose what is right, even when we have done wrong.

3

Dignity's Depth and Breadth

A human being is part of a whole, called by us the Universe, a part limited by time and space. He experiences himself, his thoughts and feelings, as something separated from the rest, a kind of optical delusion of his consciousness. This delusion is a kind of prison for us, restricting us to our personal desires and affection for a few persons nearest us. Our task must be to free ourselves from that prison by widening our circles of compassion to embrace all living creatures and the whole of nature in its beauty.

—*Albert Einstein*

Every fall, I teach a three-day weekend course entitled "Healing and Reconciling Relationships in Conflict: A Dignity Approach" at the International Center for Cooperation and Conflict Resolution at Teachers College, Columbia University, in New York City.[1] Students across the university are eligible to take the course, including those who have graduated from the university and are interested in continuing their education.

At the start of the course, I always tell my students that they already know a lot about dignity, though the course will provide participants with a language and vocabulary for talking about it. The students are encouraged to share their experiences related to dignity, and they always provide deep insight. A student in one session in particular not only described her profound experience of dignity, but also helped all of us gain a broader perspective on it.

It was the first session of the course, and the group began as usual by coming up with a working definition of dignity. We had a long discussion about what it is and what it isn't, and many of the students shared some of their experiences of having their dignity honored and violated. Everyone joined in the discussion, except for one woman, Davie Floyd, a doctoral student. In her introduction, we learned that she was a business executive on career sabbatical to get her Ph.D. in human development. She studies how to foster the development of wisdom. She saw the course offering and was curious about what a dignity approach to conflict resolution would look like. She was silent for most of the first session. It was unusual that she didn't speak. Most students are eager to share their perspectives and experience.

When I was about to take a break before starting the second session, I saw her hand go up. I was beginning to wonder what was happening with her. Was she disappointed in the material? Did she disagree with what I was presenting? What was going through her mind? I was relieved to see that she was going to make a comment and couldn't wait to hear what she had to say.

Floyd began: "Donna, I have been sitting here listening very carefully to what you and the other students have been saying about dignity. I have not contributed because I wasn't sure about how I felt, but now I know. *I think dignity is much bigger than you think it is.* You have told us that it is our inherent value and worth. That's fine, but I think it extends far beyond just our personal value. I think dignity is given to all of us as a sacred trust. It is our job to take care of and protect it, because as you said, our dignity is vulnerable. We need to think of ourselves as the guardians of dignity, but not just our own. We need to protect it in all its manifestations, in ourselves, others, and the world around us. Dignity is really about life itself, and we are all responsible for it."

Everyone sat in silence. We were stunned. I was so taken aback that all I could say was "Wow!" We all looked at her in amazement, nodding in agreement, with big smiles on our faces.

Enlightened by Floyd's insight, I have concluded that dignity can be summed up in the following way: it is about *connection, connection, and connection* (the "three Cs").

"Knowing dignity" or "dignity consciousness" means that we are connected to our own dignity (the first C), the dignity of others (the second C), and the dignity of something greater than ourselves (the third C). The third C can take on different interpretations—for some, it can mean a connection to a higher power, but it also includes a connection to the natural world and the planet that is home to us all. Additionally, it can include a connection to a purpose that contributes to the greater good—something that gives meaning to our lives.

Since I have accepted this broader perspective on dignity, I have found that a severing of any one of the three connections is a source of emotional upheaval and suffering. If we are concerned about only our own value and worth, and we fail to see the dignity of others and the world around us, we run the risk of behaving like narcissists. If we have a connection with our own and others' dignity, but we don't see the need to honor the dignity of the world we inhabit or pursue a life that contributes to the greater good, then we may suffer from a lack of meaning or purpose in our lives. This framing of dignity has helped many people see the source of their suffering and a way out of it.

As the earlier quotation by Einstein suggests, we are a part of the whole, but our ignorance of all matters related to dignity obscures the deeper connections that enable us to feel it. My husband, Rick Castino, helped me understand and experience the feeling of wholeness while we were on a trip celebrating his fiftieth birthday.

Rick loves fly fishing, and one of his favorite movies of all time is *A River Runs Through It,* a story of two brothers who spend quality time fishing in Montana. His wish for his birthday was to fish in the Gallatin River, where part of the movie had been filmed. I made all the arrangements, including finding him a river guide and a wonderful lodge for us to stay in with a majestic view of the Madison mountain range.

We arrived at the hotel after a long day of travel. We were in awe of the environment—neither of us had ever been to Montana. We got to our room, which had a lovely balcony looking directly at the mountain range. We walked out onto it; everywhere we looked was breathtaking. We stood there for a minute or two, looking straight ahead at the awe-inspiring view, and I said, "Doesn't this make you feel insignificant?" He turned to me with an incredulous look on his face and said, "Are you kidding? Insignificant? No—I feel a part of it."

What I missed when making the statement about my

insignificance in the face of the natural wonder was my own connection to dignity. Nothing should make us feel insignificant when we are connected to our inborn worth. We are all part of the wonder.

Why are the three Cs important to know for anyone trying to exercise leadership? Here's an example of how the three Cs were at play in an organization for which I was asked to conduct a dignity assessment.

A small organization that focused on immigrant issues in the United States was experiencing conflicts among its staff. The group worked tirelessly on injustices that immigrants faced in coming to the United States, doing excellent work and helping a lot of people who otherwise might not be able to afford legal services. All the employees were deeply committed to the work of the organization.

Some of the lawyers who argued the legal cases in court were older men who had been with the organization for many years. More recently, a few young women had been hired to help the legal team. The tensions had arisen between the older men and the young women lawyers. The women felt there were strong gender issues that needed to be addressed: men received the highest salaries as well as all the "perks" in the organization (for instance, they were assigned to argue the most exciting cases—those that received a lot of media attention). Some of the employees complained, too, that the workload was unfairly distributed. After some discussion, other discriminatory biases were exposed.

We determined that the following elements of dignity were being violated: *Identity* (the women felt like they were being treated differently because they were women); *Acknowledgment* (many of the people felt they suffered in silence, and no one drew attention to what they were going through); *Fair-*

ness (many felt there was a double standard around pay issues and work distribution); *Safety* (some of the employees did not feel safe to speak up when they felt their dignity was violated); and *Inclusion* (some felt left out of being considered for the more high-profile cases). It was even argued that all the elements were being violated at some point in time.

After the first day of introducing the Dignity Model to the group and articulating the dignity violations that people felt were at play in the organization, I started reflecting on how I would proceed with the second part of the work. I thought about the three Cs and realized that something fascinating was happening with the group.

I started thinking about the elements of dignity that they were trying to protect and preserve for the immigrants: *Identity* (as non-American people trying to enter the country); *Acknowledgment* (of their dire circumstances); *Fairness* (many were experiencing great injustices); *Safety* (most of them were not feeling safe and worried that at any moment they might be treated badly or even deported); and *Inclusion* (most immigrants did not experience a sense of belonging; on the contrary, they felt they lived on the margins of society). What I quickly realized was that *the very same elements of dignity that the organization's members were working righteously to protect for the immigrants, they were denying with respect to each other.* Inside the organization, they were mirroring the very violations against dignity that they were fiercely fighting on the outside.

From a three Cs perspective, they had the third C perfectly in alignment: they were working for something greater than themselves, which gave the organization its purpose and mission. Yet they were falling short on the first and second connections. Some of the staff didn't have a secure connection to their own worth. When I introduced the idea of Mandela consciousness (that dignity is in our hands alone and no one can take it away from us), many in the group admitted that they had never thought about it. The second C was also a problem because many of the employees were violating each other's dignity.

When I introduced the insight about "mirroring" to the organization, they were speechless. No one fought my interpretation. Instead, they seemed humbled by it. I held up a mirror for them, and they didn't look away. This was a remarkable group of committed individuals who wanted to create a better work environment and were willing to do what was necessary to improve their relationships with each other. The leadership team embraced the work I proposed for them. They practiced how to honor dignity, recognize when they were being lured by temptations, defend dignity (one's own and that of others), and take feedback from others. One person pointed out that even the third C, which they all related to, could improve if they got better at connecting with their own dignity and the dignity of others. To this day, the group continues to work on dignity issues inside the organization.

What made this intervention successful was that the leadership team was willing to have the mirror held up to them, even when doing so was uncomfortable. They understood their responsibility to be the guardians of dignity, of maintaining all three connections.

Dignity work is slow work, and it never ends. We all have times when we backslide, and fortunately, the Dignity Model has processes to address such times. I will describe these in detail in Part 3, but for now, the most important things to do in order to take responsibility for a dignity violation are, first, avoid pretending that it didn't happen (which is often a default reaction); instead face the person you violated and say that you are sorry. And second, because saying you are sorry is not enough, let the person know that you will commit to changing your behavior. This second step will reassure the person you harmed and remind him or her that you are a work in progress, as everyone is.

The mirroring that happened in this organization is not unique. Many groups have been struck by how their organizations suffer from the same disconnect. It is not always the case that the third C is the one that is intact and the other two are not. I have consulted in places where the first and second connections are secure, but members of the group lack a sense of purpose or a connection to something greater than themselves. The three Cs can be used as an easy diagnostic tool to see where the disconnection is happening and how to address it. No matter what, it helps to illuminate the crucial role that dignity plays in clarifying our responsibility for the well-being of the whole community, whether that community is our family, workplace, neighborhood, country, or world at large.

4

Leadership and Human Development
What Is the Connection?

What lies behind us and what lies before us are tiny matters compared to what lies within us.

—Ralph Waldo Emerson

Is it true that leadership is in a state of crisis? Are we really "waiting to be rescued," as Elizabeth Samet warned us?[1] Have we failed to develop the kind of internal confidence it takes to claim "the fountain of power" that John Adams told us we needed to secure, and then use wisely, to improve our social conditions?

I believe that, yes, we have neglected to live up to that leadership challenge. Other leadership experts are even more convinced that there is a crisis, but for different reasons. Stanford professor Jeffrey Pfeffer, author of *Leadership BS*, argues that the entire "leadership industry" is not delivering the kind of outcomes and behaviors in our leaders one might expect, given the time, energy, and resources spent on training, leadership development seminars, books, and blogs.[2]

He references multiple employee surveys and other research showing that people in the United States and around the world are "filled with dissatisfied and disengaged employees who do not trust their leaders." Workplaces, he argues, are often toxic environments that are not healthy for the people working in them, and have a negative impact on the employer company or organization as well. Yet the leadership industry, with its endless array of offerings, has not been successful in creating the kind of change within organizations that employees are yearning for.

One explanation he gives for the failure to create change is that there is little rigor in examining what works and what doesn't. He feels that the root of the problem is that the leadership industry is "so obsessively focused on the normative—what leaders should be doing and how things ought to be—that it has largely ignored asking the fundamental question of what actually is true and going on and why."

Another explanation he gives for the failure is that, more often than not, people are looking to be inspired by their leaders. It is this "preachy, feel-good approach" to leadership that has not produced the desired effects in the workplace. He argues that inspiration is not the proper foundation for accomplishing meaningful change.

I agree with Pfeffer that inspiration does not build a solid foundation for what is needed to produce the kind of change employees are looking for in their leaders and in the organizational culture. What is required instead is *insight*—insight that comes from knowing something about how to develop healthy relationships with people and about what it takes for all of us to grow and flourish.

Insight doesn't just happen. Creating a healthy social environment requires knowledge that is not typically taught in professional schools. As leadership expert Ron Heifetz points out, there is a difference between the technical work leaders are responsible for—creating a business plan, executing strategy, and using tactics necessary to achieve the vision for the company—and what he calls "adaptive work."[3] When an organization experiences problems that are not technical in nature—such as an unhappy workforce plagued by conflict or a culture that has turned toxic—leaders need to recognize that they may be at the limit of their understanding. *They need to open themselves up to new learning.* No amount of technical knowledge and expertise can fix it.

The challenges that leaders face are adaptive because they require them to push the boundaries of what they think they know, expand how they assign meaning to events, and include more of the complex human forces underlying the issues. Robert Kegan, a renowned scholar of human development, tells us that people and organizations that exceed themselves are the only ones that can meet adaptive challenges.[4] The change requires us to "get bigger" by transcending the limits of what we think we know.

The change that is needed might have something to do with leaders' own way of thinking and their own actions and behaviors, which could be causing the dysfunctional dynamics within the organization. These adaptive challenges require leaders to expand their consciousness and reduce their egocentrism. This kind of change, in turn, requires them to push themselves into a new stage of personal development—a new way of making sense of what is happening in the world around them.

By now, most people have probably heard the familiar saying by Einstein: "We cannot solve our problems with the same thinking we used when we created them." What we need is to step back and examine our own thinking and behavior, so as to understand how they might be contributing to the problems before us.

One sure way of recognizing when we are confronting the limits to the way we make meaning is to notice how often we experience problems in our relationships. What I have learned after twenty-five years of working in the field of conflict resolution is that getting into conflicts with others usually signals a need for change—change that will illuminate our blind spots and show how they are negatively affecting the people around us.

For example, a company leader called me to see whether I could help the organization with some employee problems. After interviewing both employees and members of the executive management team, it became clear that the workers felt the management team was violating their dignity by ignoring their concerns. The employees felt that they were not taken seriously and that their insight into the reasons for some conflicts wasn't being recognized as valid and helpful. The direct reports told me that they knew what was happening inside their department—the management team did not. Instead of acknowledging that they may have important data that would be useful in working out the company's problems, the executives felt "they knew better," which angered the aggrieved employees even more.

The executive team failed to ask the simple question: *What might we be doing to contribute to the problem?* Instead, they were convinced that they knew better and continued to dismiss the employees' feedback. This is a perfect example of the flawed thinking that Einstein warned us about. The managers had an opportunity to shift their thinking, but they chose not to—they decided instead to try solving the problem with the same thinking that had been used when the problem was created. The leadership failure that had led to the conflicts within the company had more to do with the failed thinking of the executives and *their lack of appreciation of their own blind spots.* By missing this opportunity to grow and develop into more complex thinkers, they became less effective leaders than if they had embraced a new approach.

Instead of thinking "we know better," a little humility would have been useful. Asking themselves "what might we not be seeing here?" would have opened the possibility that others were seeing something about their distorted thinking that they could not see. The ability to even ask that question requires an understanding of how humans develop on the inside—the kind of thinking and inner dialogue that help people make sense of themselves, others, and the world and around them. As development scholar Kegan explains, this kind of inner development takes place throughout our lifetime.[5]

If you consider the contrast between the primitive ways in which a young child understands reality and the more subtle and complex ways in which adults make meaning, it is clear that we undergo significant changes in how we think about the world and our place in it. How we grow and develop on the inside is very different from the physical changes we undergo as we mature into adults. The most significant difference is that our physical maturation ends in post-adolescence and adulthood, whereas our inner development can continue throughout our lifetime. The neuroplasticity of our brains enables us to adapt continually to new information.[6]

Even though we have the potential to develop more advanced ways of thinking throughout our lifetime, most adults fail to progress to the more complex stages. Kegan explains that the path to these higher levels of consciousness is often accompanied by a lot of inner resistance: "Just as labor pains are a part of bringing new life into the world, the process of human development, of seeing and overcoming one's previous limitations, can involve pain."[7]

Since we grow and develop in the context of relationships, they are the perfect place to test the limits of our inner development. As I mentioned earlier, if we frequently find ourselves having problems in our relationships, it is likely that we are up against a developmental challenge—in other words, *an opportunity for growth*. Recognition of how our current level of thinking (about ourselves and our relationships) is getting us into trouble can be painful because if we are operating from a blind spot, not seeing something about ourselves that others can see, the fear of humiliation or loss of face involved in owning up to it and accepting feedback may be more than we can handle. As Linda Hartling and Evelin Lindner remind us, humiliation is indeed something to fear because it puts us on a painful path of feeling isolated and disconnected from others.[8] Being that vulnerable could feel like not just a loss of face, but also, and perhaps more important, a loss of dignity. The fear and shame associated with letting go of our current way of deriving our sense of worth can be debilitating.

What might have been happening in the story about the executives and their conflict with their employees? Did they worry about how they would look in the eyes of others if they accepted that they could have been contributing to the problems the company faced? Was it possible that they acted like "they knew better" because they were fearful of admitting that they might have made a mistake? Did they resist the feedback from their employees because they couldn't tolerate what felt like a threat to their dignity? My sense is that the answer to these questions is "Yes to *all of the above.*"

To understand these dynamics, consider where the executives think their dignity comes from. I have written before about how an awareness of our dignity develops and changes over our lifetime.[9] (Or "can" change, if we understand the process and what is at stake if we don't change.) I believe that we derive and understand our dignity in three stages: dependence, independence, and interdependence.

Stage One: Dependence

When we enter the world, we are completely dependent on our caretakers for everything; infants are fragile beings, needing care and attention to survive. At this early stage, infants need to have their dignity nurtured as much as their physical needs. If children grow up in an environment where they are seen, heard, responded to, and most important, feel a sense of safety in their relationships, they will develop a healthy sense of their value and worth. At this stage, unlike when they become adults, they are dependent on their caretakers for validation of their dignity. How they are treated matters. *They experience their dignity when their caretakers treat them as worthy.* When they do not, the risk is that the child will feel unworthy. In the worst case, if someone treats the child badly, the child thinks he or she is bad. For example, a parent who is continually frustrated at work may often come home and scream at his child, even if she has done nothing wrong, or may neglect the child altogether. The child doesn't have the cognitive capacity to understand that her caretaker is taking his frustration out on her.

The child ends up feeling like she is unworthy because she feels that her worth is dependent on her caretakers' capacity to give her love and attention. The greatest vulnerability we face at this stage is not getting the external recognition we think we need to feel worthy.

Although this stage of dependence on others characterizes how children experience their worth, it is not uncommon for adults to get stuck at this developmental level. Without healthy relationships, without repeated doses of love and attention, anyone could get trapped into thinking that because others mistreat them, they must not be worthy. The need for external recognition to feel good about oneself and to have a sense of worth extends into adulthood. People still look for and derive their dignity from how others view and treat them.

Stage Two: Independence

The next stage toward developing a complete understanding of our dignity is knowing that our sense of worth depends not only on how others treat us. Building on the repeated experience of having been shown love and attention—of having our dignity honored throughout our childhood—we internalize the source of our dignity, that is, we recognize that our sense of value comes from within us. At this point, we have gained an inner confidence about ourselves that helps to ground our feelings and actions—we are not constantly looking for praise and approval to feel good. The limitation of this stage of development is that we are still vulnerable to the negative judgments of others when we think that they are questioning our value and worth. We will resist what we perceive as criticism and will fight back to preserve our dignity.

Stage Three: Interdependence

In this more evolved stage of understanding our inherent value and worth, we recognize that we do need others to protect and maintain our dignity, though not in the childlike way I have described in the dependent stage. Instead we begin to recognize that we all have limits to what we can know about ourselves, and what we might be doing that is causing trouble with others—we all have blind spots. To help us see those blind spots, and to help us gain an awareness of how we might be violating our own or others' dignity, we need extra sets of eyes. We have moved beyond simply internalizing our worth to seeing the advantage of receiving feedback from others, even if it feels uncomfortable.

As Kegan pointed out, growth can involve pain. Being able to tolerate the discomfort of having our blind spots illuminated could lead to opportunities to expand ourselves—to deepen our understanding that our worth has no limits and that our dignity is not conditional. Judgments from others do not threaten our dignity. At this stage, *we have the capacity to stay grounded in our worth and, at the same time, make ourselves vulnerable.* Even though having our blind spots illuminated by others may feel embarrassing and shameful, it does not mean we are unworthy. It simply means that it's time to grow. We recognize that we need feedback from others to develop into a more expanded version of ourselves.

We are back to where we started—needing the love and attention of others—but at this stage we need them for very different reasons. We need the love and attention not to discover our dignity, but to experience how much we are dependent on each other. In this way, we will come to understand that vulnerability is where our truth resides. Someone who cares about us and can deliver the feedback in a loving way will help us to face the potentially shameful truths of how we interact with others.

Going back to the story about the executive leadership team and the way they handled their conflicts with their employees, what did their reactions say about how they might have understood the source of their dignity? At first glance, it may have seemed like they were in the independent stage; they certainly knew that they were worthy. But they resisted the feedback of their employees and took it as criticism, which led the problems with the employees to escalate. The leadership team feared that they would lose face if they accepted the feedback of their employees. Their vulnerability to having their dignity challenged was more than they could tolerate. For this reason, the executives seem to have been trapped instead in the dependent stage, fearful that without external praise and approval, they would lose their dignity.

If, however, they were in the interdependent stage of understanding their worth, they would have been able to recognize the importance of receiving feedback from their direct reports. Instead of thinking "they knew better," they could have asked themselves, "Could we be contributing to this problem? Is it possible that the employees are right, and we are not seeing something that they can see?" They would have encouraged feedback instead of resisting it. They would have understood that their dignity was not at stake by opening themselves to a different perspective on the problem, realizing that in fact they needed their employees to hold them accountable for what they, the executives, could not see. They would have valued the feedback as an opportunity to develop a more complex and inclusive way of handling problems.

The connection between developing an advanced understanding of our dignity and our capacity to exercise effective leadership explains a lot about the "crisis" described at the beginning of the chapter. Is it possible that underlying the leadership crisis is arrested development? Is the fear of losing dignity behind some of the many leadership failures we are seeing in the world?

It should come as no surprise that the kind of development failure I highlighted earlier is common in organizations. The knowledge that is required to understand the complex human dynamics involved in maintaining a healthy sense of our worth is not usually taught in school. Something that is at the core of our shared human experience—our inherent desire to be treated with dignity—is not given the attention that it deserves by our educational system. Is it any wonder that so many leaders are unaware of the psychological impact of their actions on others and are unaware of the fragility of our inner worlds, where dignity resides?

What do all of us need to know about ourselves that would help us become better at exercising leadership, giving ourselves a wider range of options for our lives and the contributions we can make to the world?

As I mentioned earlier, one of the shocking findings in my work over the past decade has been the discovery that many people are not aware of or have failed to embrace their dignity. They are instead all too aware of feelings of inadequacy, self-doubt, and uncertainty about how good they are and how lovable they are. This is the real crisis. Instead of feeling the "fountain of power" within, they are experiencing a lack of self-confidence and, often, become powerless to effect changes in their lives. It is truly remarkable how much a little education about dignity can transform their misguided thinking about their power and capacity to act on their own behalf.

The power of dignity is something we need to be made aware of, to be responsible for, and to rejoice in. Leading an internal life without consciousness of dignity is like trying to navigate the world without a global positioning system. We need an inner compass that is grounded in the knowledge of the inherent value and vulnerability of all human beings and of the world around us.

5

How to Educate Future Leaders about Dignity

Learning about dignity has been a journey into the light of the world.

—*Student, Columbia University*

I would have never guessed that children as young as eight years old would be developmentally ready to learn about dignity. I had thought that adolescence would be a good time to start introducing the topic to students, since adolescents have a level of cognitive sophistication that would enable them to absorb these lessons. Carol Gramentine, a third-grade teacher at Trinity Valley School in Fort Worth, Texas, proved me wrong.

I had been invited to Trinity Valley School by the head of the school, Gary Krahn.[1] A mutual friend who had given him my book *Dignity* introduced us. Krahn had taken an interest in the Dignity Model and wanted to think together about how we could integrate it into the school.

Krahn is a remarkable leader in his own right. During his twenty-nine years on active duty in the U.S. Army, he served in Afghanistan and helped establish a university there. He taught mathematics at West Point, where he was the head of the Department of Mathematical Sciences. He was a brigadier general when he retired. What motivated him to become a headmaster after such a successful career in the military? Inspired by his work in Afghanistan, he realized that "habits of the heart and mind are shaped prior to the college experience." When the opportunity arose to lead Trinity Valley School, he decided to retire from the military and begin trying to "shape hearts and minds" in a K–12 setting.

After several discussions with Krahn about how to proceed with introducing the Dignity Model in the school, we decided that I would meet with members of the faculty, administration, students, and parents to present the fundamentals of the model to them. After a session with the lower-school faculty, Gramentine came up to me and told me that she felt inspired to try to develop a dignity curriculum for her third-grade students. We discussed whether they were developmentally ready. She said she couldn't be 100 percent sure, but she wanted to give it a try. She would need to make the concepts "kid friendly," in part by changing the language of the ten essential elements of dignity, but she did not see that as an obstacle.

Supported by Krahn and the lower-school principal, Sandy McNutt, Gramentine started developing the curriculum. She looked for children's books that she could use to illustrate the importance of honoring dignity, and was delighted to discover a children's version of Nelson Mandela's book *Long Walk to Freedom.* She also used Ilene Cooper's book *The Golden Rule.* After talking about dignity for a couple of weeks, referring to the books for examples, she told her students that something very exciting was going to happen: they were going to become dignity agents. The students were thrilled.

Gramentine presented questions to the students every day, and they answered them in their new "dignity journals." The first lesson began with "Introduce yourself. Write about your strengths, challenges, etc." She wanted to emphasize how important it was for students to honor their own dignity and be proud of who they were. In addition to writing, she encouraged them to draw pictures to represent what they felt.

The next question was to ask themselves at the end of the day how their actions and behaviors made others feel. "Did you make people feel happy or sad? If so, what did you do?" Everybody, including Gramentine, answered in their journals. At the end of the day, the students were encouraged to share their thoughts with the class. Gramentine shared her writings as well. When she admitted that she might have made someone feel bad, she wrote that she needed to apologize to the person whose dignity she had violated. Her modeling made it easy for the students to come forward with their experiences. They saw that their teacher didn't expect them to be perfect; instead she wanted them to become aware of how their behavior affects others, positively or negatively.

Gramentine's curriculum was filled with thoughtful questions and exercises. All the elements of dignity were described in words that the kids could grasp. For example, "acceptance of identity" became "everyone matters"; "inclusion" became "make others feel that they belong"; and "benefit of the doubt" became "believe in people."

After the students learned the elements, they wrote them on the board at the front of the classroom, and every morning they would review them. Gramentine would also ask whether anyone had observed any of the elements in use. The students would then tell stories about what they had seen—either a violation or an honoring of dignity. All day long, if a dignity issue arose, the class would use it as a teaching and learning opportunity.

The last part of the training involved sharing what the students had learned with others. Gramentine set up sessions with two first-grade classes, and the principal, assistant principal, counselor, a learning specialist, and others participated. Her group of students was divided into two groups, each of which was to describe an element of dignity by drawing a picture of the element on a poster board, writing what the element meant, and coming up with an example they had observed when the element had either been honored or violated. The students were completely in charge of how they wanted to present their work. It was a huge success.

Gramentine was astonished by the extent to which the students had grasped and internalized the elements of dignity. Their mastery was especially apparent during the question-and-answer period with the audience, when their answers confirmed to her that, without a doubt, third-graders were capable of understanding dignity and the impact it has on their lives and relationships. Even though they may not have been as cognitively mature as adolescents, it really didn't matter because they knew how it felt to have dignity honored or violated. I was soon to learn that children as young as five years old can grasp the feeling of what happens to their dignity.

Carol Gramentine remains committed to teaching dignity to her students. She recently wrote to me about a student who was totally transformed by her dignity teachings:

> He is a kid who has had serious behavior issues, trouble with self-control, difficulties getting along with peers, anger and anxiety since kindergarten. He has had quite a good year with me but has still struggled quite often, until . . . we started our dignity study. His parents say he is a new child. I have made him the master dignity agent and spokesperson for our class. He (a kid who never liked to write) has filled two complete journals with his thoughts on dignity. It brings me to tears at times thinking of his transformation. I could go on and on.[2]

She has many stories like this one. Carol's vision to create a dignity curriculum for her students became a reality, and because of her efforts, many third-graders will not wait until they are adults to engage in meaningful leadership.

After our work together, Gary Krahn left Trinity Valley School and moved to San Diego, California, to address some urgent family issues. Everyone at Trinity Valley was sad to see him go, and it didn't take long for him to find another position at the La Jolla Country Day School in San Diego.[3]

Krahn invited me to come to La Jolla Country Day School to replicate the work we had done at Trinity Valley. We took a similar approach to introducing the Dignity Model by having me talk to the faculty, administration, students, and parents. He was determined to establish a culture of dignity in the school. It was an easy sell, since the school was filled with inspiring and thoughtful faculty and administrators who were eager to learn about my dignity work. After I made a couple of trips to work with all of them, they were ready to start integrating dignity concepts into their curriculum.[4]

As surprised as I was to hear of Carol Gramentine's success with her third graders at Trinity Valley School, I was even more shocked to learn that Martha Migdal at La Jolla had integrated dignity teachings into her junior kindergarten class. Martha's approach is to stress that *every person matters*. She does this by encouraging her students to share, take turns, listen, be aware of others' feelings, and include others in play. She said that another important component of her dignity work is modeling how to treat the children with dignity. She believes it is the best way to help them learn how to treat themselves and others. Teachers are powerful role models.

Second-grade teachers Beth Levin, Julie Mindel, Alisa Ronis, and Molly Saenz report that they teach dignity lessons every day in class. It is modeled through role playing and literature. The students are encouraged to reflect on their behaviors and to see how their words and actions affect others. These teachers also believe that modeling dignified behaviors is key for second graders.

Third-grade teacher Lisa Bennet explains that dignity, respect, and kindness are the foundational elements on which their classroom communities are built. Their goal is to ensure that the classroom environment is safe for everyone and is a place where children can feel free to express themselves and to be who they are. They use literature as a tool to help the students think about dignity and how dignity affects the characters in the story line. With the language of dignity, the children come to understand injustice when they see it in other settings and other parts of the world. Lisa reports that since the children have been equipped with their new understanding of the importance of dignity, they have become more empathic toward others and aware of their inherent value. They are also well prepared to live up to their own human potential.

Kristy Johnson, assistant head of the middle school at La Jolla Country Day School, explains that the advisory period is used to introduce dignity to their students. The advisory period is a time for the middle-schoolers to meet with their adviser (a faculty member) and come together as a group to discuss topics such as diversity, inclusivity, dignity, and health and wellness. Students are asked to create their own under-standing of the essential elements of dignity. Once they have a good idea of what dignity is, they talk about times when they felt it had been honored or violated. They are asked to identify their dignity strengths and weaknesses and to highlight issues they would like to work on in their relationships with others.

The goal of Nate Heppner, an eighth-grade English teacher, is to use literature and writing as a lens through which students can examine dignity issues. He has found that most characters have both "dignity ups and downs," and so accurately repre-sent what most of us go through in our lives as we try to honor our own dignity and that of others.

Jonathan Shulman, the history department chair, uses the dignity frame in many of his projects with students as a guide for conversation and reflection on important aspects of world history. Every ninth grader completes an oral history project that contains ideas from the Dignity Model. The model provides direction for the student in finding a deeper philo-sophical purpose for their personal project.

Cortney Golub, a history teacher in the upper school, ex-plains that dignity is the heart and soul of her classroom cul-ture. Rephrasing a quote by Maya Angelou, she says, "Students will remember how you and your class culture made them feel more so than the content that was learned." She makes sure that she gives her love and acceptance to every student. Former students who had been in her class have told her, "I loved your class because of the way it was constructed and taught and because you treated and honored us with love and dignity." She said that when students are treated with dignity, they feel safe to "be wrong" because everyone sees themselves as equally vulnerable individuals working on becoming their authentic selves: "That is the value of using the lens of dignity in education."

Jane Healey, a member of the upper-school faculty, says that teaching history and literature without a dignity lens reduces human events and artifacts to names, dates, and locations. "Teaching with dignity" humanizes history and current events.

Blair Overstreet is part of the upper-school faculty and is the new faculty coordinator. During a week-long orientation, the new faculty were introduced to the Dignity Model and learned how it has been integrated into the culture at La Jolla Country Day School. In their evaluations, the new teachers reported that they found the dignity sessions the most meaningful part of their introductory presentations.

Cindy Bravo, a member of the upper-school arts faculty and coordinator of a group called Diversity Advocates, describes the dignity elements as the inner core that maintains our spiritual balance and holds our psychological posture upright and flexible in life. In her work as diversity coordinator, she points out that honoring the elements of dignity in every human being would lead to a higher state of consciousness about how we come together to enrich each other's lives as people of differing ethnicities, sexualities, socioeconomic backgrounds, and abilities.

Robin Stewart, a member of the upper-school humanities faculty and the inclusivity coordinator, teaches literature and philosophy. She says that she presents the students with works by authors and philosophers who have guided generations before them as a way to help the students recognize and reflect on their shared humanity, and grasp and grapple with dignity. One of her maxims is "shame never creates change."

Colleen O'Boyle, the assistant head of school for academic affairs, says that the school empowers students intellectually, socially, and emotionally by cultivating a space, using the dignity elements, in which knowledge, acceptance, understanding, and care are used when discussing matters important to the self and community. Inez Odom, the assistant head of school for enrollment management and outreach, has stressed the importance of having faculty, administrators, and parents model dignified behaviors.

Sixth-grader Shannon White sums it up this way: "In my opinion, dignity is the closest thing one has to being of nobility even if they aren't royal. It's what makes us stand tall even when our greatest desire is to fall."

These accounts of the application of the Dignity Model into the curriculum and culture, from the lower school to upper school, show the commitment and determination of Gary Krahn, his remarkable faculty, and the school administrators to establish a culture of dignity at La Jolla Country Day School.

Another extraordinary educator, Mike Wilper, who teaches history and English at Berkeley Carroll School in Brooklyn, New York, has effectively integrated dignity lessons into his classes with middle school students.[5] This is what Mike said about how he incorporates dignity into his teachings:

We weave the concept of universal human dignity through all of our units in history and English. We begin with a pledge to the students that we will not humiliate them, that we will always be honest with them, and that we will always believe in them. We then introduce the concept of universal human dignity and the simple yet profound idea that we all deserve to be treated well and in turn are obliged to treat others well.

While setting up these expectations and norms in the room, we also begin building out the concept of dignity intellectually. We start with learning the essential elements of dignity. We also introduce a basic critical thinking vocabulary centered on the fallacies and biases that too often lead us to rely on weak inferences and hasty generalizations about other people. We then spend time contemplating the complexity and profound potential of every individual. We look at the underlying reasons why some of us struggle (fixed mindsets, anti-achievement subcultures, overwhelmed cognitive loads) and why others flourish (growth mindset, adaptive strategies, deliberate practice). We see that every individual faces a vast array of obstacles and opportunities (the ten temptations to violate dignity), most of which remain hidden unless you take the time to really look for them. Understanding the complexity of every individual allows us to cultivate empathy and perspective-taking. We offer multiple opportunities to role play, both in small set pieces related to the history or literary content we are studying and in multiple-day projects that require students to navigate a complex conflict.

Some days they might be Roman governors and provincial subjects hashing out a regional government. Other days, they are asked to negotiate a mock social conflict involving an escalating revenge cycle, unrequited love, or online bullying. By recognizing the dignity of everyone, especially the need for safety, autonomy, connection, and purpose, the students learn that we all often react blindly to the conflicts that arise in our lives, and that the best bet is almost always to sift through the underlying issues, feelings, and misunderstandings.

We use the concept of dignity as a platform to teach students how to engage in difficult conversations. How do you disagree with someone and maintain a sense of goodwill? How do you let someone know they've hurt you without accusing the person of malevolence? By equipping our students with this toolkit, they walk through the community spaces differently. They are more conscious of the dignity of others and the impact of their actions. We also ask them to evaluate the broader culture of our communities, analyzing commercials, TV shows, and other media outlets to "measure" how the content we consume impacts our sense of how we think of ourselves as people who are complex and inherently valuable.

As the students move into the wider world, they are equipped to become leaders who are conscious of dignity. If we hope to teach young people to become strong leaders, we would do well to emphasize the need to listen to others, to recognize their dignity needs and complexities, and to help them solve problems. The dignity work helps students see leadership not as an exercise in personal ego, but rather as an opportunity to contribute to the well-being of others and the world around them.

Here is what one of Wilper's students wrote about his dignity education:

> After a year with Mr. Wilper, I learned dignity was more than just being nice to people. It incorporates so many more aspects. It is compassion, inclusivity, and most of all, acceptance. The true test of dignity is to treat people as equal, without focusing on the fact that they have a different skin color or if they are gay. Learning about dignity helped me so much in all aspects of my life. I was given a lens to see the world differently. If more people my age were given this lens, we would become a better generation. Our generation could help fix the world, even at our age.

Another student wrote:

> Mr. Wilper's class taught me about current problems in our society that I was only vaguely aware of before. But one of the most impacting subjects I learned about last year was dignity, how it can be violated, and the issues that violation of dignity can lead to. I don't think it goes too far to say that

learning about dignity changed my perspective on the world. My classmates and I used to say that we had learned more in the past year than we had in all of our other school years combined. Although this statement is a bit exaggerated, there is much truth to it. Thank you, Mr. Wilper.[6]

These inspiring stories from Trinity Valley School, La Jolla Country Day School, and Berkeley Carroll School have given me reason to believe that learning about dignity—our own, the dignity of others, and the dignity of the world around us—brings out the leadership potential in our children. Dignity education seems to inspire these young people not just to treat everyone with recognition that they matter, but also to see their own capacity to make a difference in the world.

When students develop a secure connection to their own dignity—realizing their inherent value and worth—it frees them from self-doubt and the worrying question "Am I good enough?" When students recognize that they are good enough, no matter what, their hearts and minds are free to explore the possibility of living a life that has meaning and purpose, making the world a more loving and accepting home for us all.

II
What You Need to Do to Lead with Dignity

We are all born with dignity; we're just not born knowing how to act like it.

6

Demonstrate and Encourage Lifelong Learning and Development

The passion for stretching yourself and sticking to it, even (or especially) when it's not going well, is the hallmark of the growth mindset. This is the mindset that allows people to thrive during some of the most challenging times in their lives.
—*Carol Dweck*

Understanding that learning and development have no expiration dates could be one of the most important messages for promoting well-being and our ability to realize the potential for growth that resides within us all. Anyone who exercises leadership, from the very top of an organization or within it, will benefit from this insight.

As Kenneth Robinson notes in his co-authored book *Creative Schools,* "Human beings are highly curious learning organisms."[1] He points out that even though we have a voracious appetite for learning, it is not uncommon for children to lose that deep curiosity during their educational experience. His work details the kind of educational reform that is necessary to keep the desire for learning alive. Although it is not within the scope of this book to explore this vital aspect of education, he makes one other point that is directly related to lifelong learning and dignity:

> As human beings, we all live in two worlds. There is the world that exists whether you exist or not. It was there before you came into it and it will be there when you have gone. This is the world of objects, events and other people; it is the world around you. There is another world that exists only because you exist: the private world of your own thoughts, feelings and perceptions; the world within you.

If we fail to understand and pay attention to this rich, influential, and often punishing aspect of our inner worlds—the place where our dignity resides—we run the risk of a great deal of silent human suffering. The content of the dialogue that takes place inside often determines how we feel about ourselves, others, and the world external to us. This inner dialogue constantly monitors the self in relation to others and asks, "Am I good enough, smart enough, and lovable enough?" This dialogue, in turn, determines who we think we are and what we are capable of.

The greatest danger in not being acquainted with the world within is that if we let it go unmonitored and unsupervised, its default is set for self-doubt, not for self-compassion. If we are not taught to realize the untapped potential within us, and that our starting point is one of love and dignity, our inner life will be fraught with turbulence and despair. As Thoreau said, "The mass of men lead lives of quiet desperation, and go to the grave with the song still in them."[2] (Of course, the same is true of women.) What a waste of potential, a barrier to learning, and an impediment to living life to its fullest.

Getting stuck in this kind of mindset is damaging not only to us individually, but to society as well. Think of the difference we could all make if we knew, from a very young age, that we had the potential to contribute to the well-being of the world as well as to our own personal fulfillment. Learning that we are capable of learning and growing throughout our lives requires an inner dialogue that is set for self-compassion, not self-doubt.

Carol Dweck has advanced this idea in her seminal book *Mindset: The New Psychology of Success.*[3] After years of research, Dweck discovered that the way we think about ourselves strongly influences how we lead our lives. She tells us that most people have either a "fixed mindset" or a "growth mindset," which determines how smart we think we are, how capable we are, and whether we think we can change. If we have a "fixed mindset," we think of ourselves and our personal attributes in predetermined ways—I'm not smart, or I'm not creative, or I'm not likable and there's nothing I can do to change it.

A "growth mindset," in contrast, recognizes our potential and understands that we can do many things if we put our mind to it. With practice and effort, we are capable of developing many new qualities and attributes. These mindsets are the content of our inner dialogue and can affect the way we conduct our lives and our openness to learning. Most importantly, a growth mindset can encourage us to keep going, even when setbacks occur. A "failure" only means we must do something differently. It doesn't mean we are a failure.

Carol also points out that the fixed mindset creates barriers to learning. If you think you are not smart, you give up and don't try harder. A growth mindset, however, encourages people to look for opportunities to learn new things. The internal barriers are absent. The difference between the two can be summed up in this question: *Am I smart or am I learning?*

It seems that there is a link between consciousness of dignity and the growth mindset. Having an awareness of, and connection to, one's inherent value and worth could be the anchor we need to tolerate the pains and enjoy the pleasures of a growth mindset. We can be much freer to take risks and make ourselves vulnerable when we know that our sense of value and worth is intact—when we have achieved the Mandela consciousness that I described in the Introduction. This consciousness helps when we are confronted with obstacles and setbacks, enabling us to bounce back and show resilience. If we are not worried about our worth, a lot of space is freed up for self-expansion and development.

The fixed mindset, with its "either/or" framing of who we think we are, sets the stage for questioning our worth. As Dweck points out, people with a fixed mindset think in terms of being inferior or superior to others. Not only are they quick to negatively judge themselves; they are continually judging others as well. They appear not to have a strong sense of the inviolable truth of their worth. She says that parents who have a fixed mindset that they pass along to their children measure their kids' worth by how smart they are, not by their openness to learning.

This is a problem. Early on, the content of their children's inner dialogue—their assessment of their worth and their ability to be open to learning—is arrested. Their worth is conditional—they need to be smart to feel good about who they are. It is easy to see how this groundwork contributes to the crisis in development that I referred to earlier. Is it any wonder that we are not ready to think of ourselves as leaders?

If we want to exercise leadership, what do we have to do to communicate the importance of a growth mindset—one that measures success by our willingness to stay open to learning, even when it feels uncomfortable? First and foremost, we need to demonstrate our connection to our own dignity. We need to have Mandela consciousness. Without being firmly rooted in our own inherent value and worth, we run the risk of

- Being destabilized by any problem or negative judgments that come our way
- Taking feedback as criticism rather than a growth opportunity
- Having false dignity—thinking that our worth comes from external validation in the form of praise and approval
- Being reactive rather than reflective
- Falling prey to the ten temptations to violate our own dignity

Without Mandela consciousness (the "I," with its expansive notion of what we are capable of), we allow *survival consciousness* (the "Me") to rule our inner worlds. Our "Me" takes charge, looking for recognition of our dignity outside of ourselves. We are limited by the need to be seen in a favorable light. This comes at a great cost; when we are dependent on others to feel good about who we are, staying open to learning means we risk not getting external validation. What if being open to learning means that we recognize the need to change, potentially upsetting what we think the world expects of us?

When we are "Me" dominated, we are not open to feedback from others—it feels too much like criticism. We are not able to learn from mistakes because we think they expose our incompetence. We are not able to tolerate the ongoing instability that being open to new learning creates. When we are constantly worried about appearing smart enough, good enough, and capable enough, opening ourselves up to new learning could be a threat to the erratic sense of worth that haunts the internally unstable "Me."

These are all big challenges that we face if and when we decide to lead with dignity. It means we need to get comfortable with uncertainty, vulnerability, and the potential pushback we could receive by challenging the status quo of our understanding of who we are and what our organization needs to continue to grow and flourish. As I have described earlier, this is what Ron Heifetz means by adaptive work: embracing the kind of work that pushes the boundaries of what we know and being willing to hold steady in the face of the resistance to it. Bob Kegan reminds us that being open to learning and development often involves pain. The task of good leadership is to manage the pain in such a way that the people involved feel reassured that the only path forward is to go through it and to do it together.

Staying connected to each other and the larger purpose of the organization (here is where the three Cs come into the picture again) enables everyone to reap the benefits of staying open to learning. It provides *a new and expanded understanding of who we are, what we think we are capable of, and how that expanded consciousness contributes to fulfilling the purpose of the organization.* As Dweck pointed out in the quotation that opened this chapter, the times when we stretch ourselves, even when it feels uncomfortable, are when we experience the greatest opportunity for growth. Susan David tells us that this kind of emotional agility is what makes it possible to stay open to keeping growth alive and well throughout our lifetimes.[4]

Staying open to lifelong learning requires anyone who wants to exercise leadership to

- *Be aware of the content of your inner dialogue.* Does it reflect an awareness of your inherent value and worth? Is your dialogue "Me" driven or is it firmly rooted in your "I"?
- *Watch for judgments about what you are capable of.* When you are unsuccessful at achieving a goal or make a mistake, what do you tell yourself? Beware of the impulse to hijack your own learning process. Ask yourself: Even if I made a mistake, am I still learning?
- *Be curious.* Look for opportunities to expand your understanding of yourself and the world around you. Recognize that the more you know, the more you will see what you don't know.
- *Eliminate the word* failure *from your self-assessment.* A "failure" means only that you must do something differently.

Is it possible to run a business or an organization that has, as part of its purpose, a commitment to providing an ongoing learning environment for its people? Robert Kegan and Lisa Laskow Lahey have spent their careers as scholars and as organizational consultants researching this question. In their new book *An Everyone Culture: Becoming a Deliberately Developmental Organization,* they have concluded that it is possible.[5] They showcase three businesses that have a commitment to building a work environment where everyone's growth and development is a priority. These businesses discovered that realizing organizational potential is about realizing human potential.

Kegan and Lahey start their book with the provocative idea that people in organizations are doing two jobs: the first is the one that they were hired to do, and the second one, which is often a bigger energy drain than the first, involves trying to cover up their weaknesses, managing how they think others see them, and trying to look the best they can in the eyes of others. They say that this second job is about *hiding*: hiding aspects of the authentic self, including inadequacies and perceived limitations. The thought of exposing these vulnerabilities is terrifying.

From a dignity perspective, it sounds as if Kegan and Leahy are talking about people who are driven by their "Me." Such persons are overly concerned about how they appear in the eyes of others, fearful of exposing what they don't know, and too reliant on external recognition of their value and worth. In short, they are afraid of looking unworthy.

Would a safer environment enable their people to shift from a "Me"-driven survival consciousness to a Mandela consciousness so that they would be more likely to feel their unconditional worth and let their "I" dominate their thinking? Would a learning environment where people felt free to expose their limitations help push them beyond their comfort zone to an expanded understanding of themselves and the world around them?

The three organizations that Kegan and Lahey featured in their book have done just that—they have created environments where people are free to be their authentic selves, without fear of judgment, paving the way for their ongoing growth. They are called *deliberately developmental organizations.*

You may wonder whether it is really the task of organizations to promote the development of their people. Won't that take away from the growth potential of the organization? The results have shown that the opposite is true. The authors report that the benefits associated with creating a deliberately developmental organization include

- An increase in profitability, improved employee retention, faster promotions, more frank communication, improved error detection in operational and strategic design, more effective delegation, and enhanced accountability
- Reductions in cost structures, political maneuvering, interdepartmental strife, employee downtime, and disengagement
- Solutions to seemingly intractable problems, such as how to convert a team of leaders (each looking out for his or her own franchise) into a more valuable, but elusive, leadership team; how to anticipate and weather crises that no one in the company has experienced before; and how to invent and realize future possibilities

A key factor in establishing a deliberately developmental organization is acknowledging the power of each member's inner dialogue and how it can change and develop into more complex ways of understanding both the individual and the world at large—in short, of understanding that this dialogue can be "improved and managed." Wise leaders know that exposing the contents of our inner lives is essential to our growth process. Instead of fearing that we will be negatively judged for showing what we feel are our limitations and weaknesses, we need to get comfortable with showing them to the world.

To make possible this openness and all the opportunities it presents, the leadership team of the organization must communicate, through their actions and behavior, *that it is safe to be vulnerable.* They need to set the tone and demonstrate what it looks like to overcome our natural reluctance to open ourselves up to the possibility of losing face and the experience of shame that goes along with it. Overcoming our hardwired instincts to protect ourselves from looking bad in the eyes of others is difficult—we don't want to appear weak. But with dignity consciousness, we learn that vulnerability is far from weakness; it is where truth resides. It requires far more strength to embrace the truth and resist the temptations to cover it up than it does to try to hide from it.

7

Set the Tone

Make It Safe to Be Vulnerable

Vulnerability is the core, the heart, the center, of meaningful human experiences.

—*Brené Brown*

To create an environment where people will feel open to further learning and development, those in leadership positions should encourage and model this openness. The foundation for this approach is a keen awareness of how vulnerable we are as human beings to having our dignity violated and how such violations create obstacles to learning and productivity. Reacting to and recovering from wounds to our dignity occupy precious time and space in our inner worlds; the suffering they create puts our growth on hold.

Armed with these insights, those in leadership positions need to realize what an honor it is to be a guardian of dignity.

It should be a privilege reserved for those who have something important to offer humanity in our quest to evolve and become the most of what we are capable of. Helping people develop their capacity to connect with one another in a way that promotes mutual growth and well-being is a tall order. Yet it is essential work, for we cannot evolve in isolation and alienation from one another. Jean Baker Miller, who first proposed the relational model of human development, reminds us that growth-fostering relationships are a central human necessity. Human development occurs in the context of relationships.[1] Creating an environment that acknowledges the importance of healthy human connections—where the three Cs define the goals and aspirations of how to be together—starts with those in leadership positions.

Leaders set the tone in organizations. They have the power to affect how people feel on a moment-by-moment basis. Whether they are aware of it or not, employees scrutinize every move they make, taking cues from them to determine what is acceptable and unacceptable in the way they interact at work. Yet in interviewing leaders, I have found that *they are often unaware of the extent to which their actions and behaviors set the norms for the work environment.*

One manager, for example, was shocked to learn from her direct reports how violating it felt for them when she came into the office and never said "good morning" to anyone. Every day, she would walk by them with her head down, avoiding even eye contact. To the people she walked past, her failure to greet them meant that she didn't care enough about them to say hello. *Even when we are not speaking, we're communicating.* The message the manager was sending was that people aren't important—just get the work done. The environment was filled with unspoken resentment.

The manager had no idea that she was having such an effect on her people. She never gave it a thought that she might be signaling that they weren't important. She explained that she felt overwhelmed all the time with her job responsibilities. Her mind was always on her work—what she needed to do, and how little time she felt she had to accomplish all her tasks. Did she intend to make the people she managed feel that she didn't care about them? Of course she didn't. Even so, they felt she was not really seeing them.

This manager's experience illustrates why we need to pay more attention to the effect we have on others. *Without dignity consciousness, even good people with good intentions can cause harm.*

As I mentioned earlier, the vast majority of people in leadership positions whom I have interviewed are good people. They simply knew little about dignity and were unaware how much we all want the kind of human connection that even a simple smile and hello can accomplish. In fact, a smile communicates more than just a simple greeting. It is one of the most ancient ways that we communicate safety.[2] It is an exchange that has its roots deep in our evolutionary heritage. Try smiling at a stranger and see how often the smile is returned. We are hardwired to respond positively to a smile.

I have conducted hundreds of interviews with employees in a variety of work settings, assessing the ways in which they felt their dignity was being honored and violated. Across all settings, the element of dignity that was violated the most was safety. *People did not feel safe to speak up to their bosses when they felt uncomfortable with the way they were being treated.* They were fearful that if they made themselves vulnerable by telling their supervisors about how they felt violated, they would get a poor performance review or even lose their jobs.

They would tell me that making themselves vulnerable would be "career suicide."

The research of Harvard Business School professor Amy Edmundson demonstrates the importance of creating a "psychologically safe" environment in the workplace.[3] Her findings indicate that when people feel safe working with others, their capacity for learning and performance increases significantly. Safety also predicts the employees' engagement and the quality of work produced.[4]

How do leaders make it safe to be vulnerable? This is the most challenging work I do with organizations. The easier work is helping leaders to understand how to honor dignity, how to be mindful of the temptations to violate our own dignity, and how to implement all the other aspects of dignity leadership. Most leaders welcome these insights and are eager to learn. But when I explain how important it is for the well-being of the people (and the organization) that everyone feel safe to speak up when something doesn't feel right about the way they are being treated, it usually elicits a look of panic. What? You want me to have feedback sessions with my people so that they can let me know when I have violated their dignity? I can't do that!

We have a strong resistance to feedback. In *Thanks for the Feedback: The Science and Art of Receiving Feedback Well*, Douglas Stone and Sheila Heen describe the neuroscience behind the resistance.[5] They explain that when our brain detects the possibility of danger, there is an automatic response. One of the most ancient parts, the amygdala (where the emotions center resides) is activated, and tells us to either fight or flee to avoid the potential harm. Quoting psychologist Jonathan Haidt: "threats get a shortcut to your panic button," which is why our reaction to negative feedback feels so automatic.

This immediate response to threatening situations explains why each of the ten temptations—in this case, the temptation to resist feedback—is so hard to overcome. The fight to preserve the self is fierce, even if, in principle, people know that it will help them in their relationships with their employees. But there is a clue in this resistance; *the more that people fight the feedback, the more it tells me how they derive their sense of dignity.* Are they terrified that if they receive negative feedback, it will challenge their sense of worth? Are they relying on external praise and approval to derive their dignity? Are they in the dependent stage? Are they aware that their dignity is in their hands only (*independent stage*) but are not all that comfortable with receiving feedback? Or, ideally, do they have Mandela consciousness? Are they at the *interdependent stage,* in which they understand the need for input from others to illuminate the blind spots that we all have that are getting us into trouble in our relationships? Do they recognize that without the help of others to help them see what they cannot see, they run the risk of violating not only their own dignity but also the dignity of those around them? Do we need our leaders to be in this interdependent stage of dignity awareness to lead with dignity?

Emotionally, feedback is risky business. Without the internal anchor that comes with Mandela consciousness, feedback, especially feedback that feels threatening to our sense of worth, can trigger a strong fear response. If we are held together on the inside by praise and approval from outside of ourselves, our self-preservation instincts will take over when feedback is offered because it may feel like our survival is on the line, even if of course it is not. If, however, we know that our dignity is in our hands only, and our worth is not on the line, then we will be more open to hearing what others have to say about how we might be compromising our own dignity and harming others in the process.

Why is being open to feedback important for leaders to demonstrate and model? Stone and Heen tell us that those who are open to feedback, who engage in "feedback-seeking behaviors," have higher job satisfaction, enjoy greater creativity on the job, adapt more quickly in a new organization or role, and have lower turnover. In particular, they say, seeking *negative* feedback is associated with higher job performance. They also make clear that "nothing affects the learning culture of an organization more than the skill with which its executive team receives feedback."

I try to explain to people in leadership positions that when their employees feel violated—and then feel unsafe in the presence of those who have violated them—trust is shattered and they disconnect from the relationship. The second of the three Cs is severed. It is a matter of self-protection. No one wants to leave himself or herself open to the possibility of being hurt again.

What may be obvious, but important to point out, is that this disconnection happens even though people still must work together. Instead of having a relationship in which everyone feels safe and free to be their true selves, resentment builds, and people are always on guard for the next attack. The relationship exists, but it no longer promotes a feeling of safety and authentic connection.

Restoring the connection requires the person violating dignity to take action. The first step is to realize that it doesn't really matter whether the perpetrator *intended* to cause harm. As Melanie Tannenbaum points out in the *Scientific American Blog Network*, the perpetrator's *intent* is not as important as the impact of the action.[6] "Was someone hurt by something?

Was there a negative outcome? Did someone suffer? If so, that is what is important. Whether the perpetrator meant to cause the harm is not." That being said, she also makes the point that although unintended harms are damaging, people judge perpetrators more harshly if they think that they intentionally tried to inflict harm than if they think they did it unintentionally.

It is critical for people in leadership positions to understand the distinction between intentions and impact. It is also important to understand the inherent resistance we all have to receiving feedback and how it is necessary to take the first steps in demonstrating a commitment to it. In this case, leading with dignity requires leaders to set the tone by asking for feedback and modeling what is expected.

Here are some steps that can be taken to make it safe for such feedback to be given and received:

- Make it clear to your employees that you value their feedback and that you will make it a routine part of your relationship with them.
- Explain that the purpose of feedback is to promote a learning environment for everyone in the organization.
- Acknowledge that it will be difficult in the beginning because we all have built-in resistance to both giving feedback and receiving it.
- Explain that there are ways to both give and receive feedback that will require some learning to overcome this resistance.
- Explain that there will most likely be a growth curve in everyone's ability to feel comfortable giving and receiving feedback.
- Make it clear that no one will be penalized for giving feedback.

Once leaders have set the stage for giving and receiving feedback, explaining that it is a way for the organization to create opportunities for all people to grow in their jobs, the next step is to prepare everyone for how to both give it and receive it.

To illustrate this next step, consider my earlier story about the manager who had no idea that by not saying hello to her employees when she came to work in the morning, she was violating their dignity and sending the message that the only important thing was "getting the work done."

In preparation for a feedback session with the manager, I first worked with those whom she was ignoring when she arrived. I needed to help them develop the skills necessary to give the feedback in a way that the manager could hear it. The first lesson was to *give the feedback in a way that allows the person receiving it to hear it as an opportunity to learn something about herself.* When feedback is delivered as a weapon, as a way to get back at or get even with the person who violated you, the person receiving the feedback is likely to get defensive and will not be open to what you have to say.

When I worked with this group, we discussed the violation they felt (the manager never said hello or acknowledged them when she came into the office, and they perceived this as her showing them that she felt they were unimportant). Discussing it helped to diffuse the resentment they felt and helped them get their "I," instead of their reactive "Me," into the driver's seat. It's difficult to talk about a dignity violation if you are still feeling the sting of it.

I suggested that they use language like: "We are giving you feedback because our relationship with you is important to us. We all want a good work environment, and we are sure you do, too. Also, what we have to tell you is a small part of who you are as our manager. There are many things about our job and your leadership that we are happy about (list a few things here)." They would then let her know how they experienced her lack of a greeting or eye contact when she came into the office in the morning.

The job of the manager is to listen carefully, then acknowledge the concern. "Now that you are telling me about my failure to greet you, I can see how it would be upsetting to all of you and that it sent the wrong message." Her final remark should be a sincere apology. "I'm really sorry that I haven't communicated how important you all are to this organization. I couldn't do this job without you. Thank you for your honesty and willingness to help me see something that was in my blind spot."

Even though people are generally fearful of feedback sessions, my experience is that if they are done right—as I have described here—the relationship ends up not only repaired, but stronger. There is something powerful that happens when a person is given feedback—especially if it is something about her or his behavior that the receiver is not aware of. When the receiver is not defensive—doesn't give excuses or simply respond that the action wasn't intended to be hurtful—and is open to learning, it has a healing effect on the people or person giving the feedback. It is my sense that when someone honestly apologizes for hurtful behavior, empathy is restored. We know what courage it takes to not be defensive and to hold oneself accountable. We are moved by such strength. For this reason, those who have been violated frequently want to respond to the apology with, "Oh, that's okay." In that moment, though, it is important for the givers of the feedback to say instead, in an acknowledgment of everyone's effort to get to that point: "Thank you for that apology—it means a lot to us."

Demonstrating your willingness to receive and use even

difficult-to-hear feedback sends many positive messages beyond the simple act of listening to the feedback without resisting it. It tells people that you are strong enough to hear it—that
your sense of your worth is not threatened by their concerns.
It tells people that what they have to say matters to you, that
you know that they have a perspective that you do not have
and that your own growth and development are dependent on
their honesty and courage. And it says that what matters most
to you is the truth about how people experience you, not some
false appearance that requires deceit and deception to maintain and defend.

Bringing out the best and most authentic version of ourselves requires a willingness to be vulnerable. As Brown's quotation at the beginning of the chapter explains, "Vulnerability
is the core, the heart, the center, of meaningful human experiences."[7] It makes one wonder why we have resisted it for so
long.

8

Cultivate Trust

Trust is the lubrication that makes it possible for organizations to work.

—*Warren Bennis*

Another benefit of making it safe to be vulnerable within organizations is that it creates trust—an essential ingredient in healthy relationships. Research has shown that when people trust each other at work because their relationships are strong, they are more committed to the organization and more willing to make a positive contribution.[1] Other research has shown that interpersonal trust is necessary to the functioning of organizations and plays a role in determining whether they achieve their goals and objectives. Trust also helps build employee commitment and increases the reputation of the organization, as well as organizational performance.[2]

In an article in the *Harvard Business Review*, Stephen Covey and Douglas Conant argue that "trust is not a soft, social virtue—it is truly a hard, economic driver for every organization."[3] They explain that Great Place to Work's report on the "100 Best Companies to Work For" found that "trust between managers and employees is the primary defining characteristic of the very best workplaces." They added: "These companies beat the average annualized returns of the S&P 500 by a factor of three."

What these researchers are telling us about the importance of trust in the practice of good leadership should not surprise us. We all know intuitively that trust is necessary for authentic relationships, yet we also know how fragile it is and how easily it can be destroyed. What role does dignity play in the development of and in the destruction of trust? Let me share a story that demonstrates the critical role it plays in both.

As is usually the case, I was invited into a company to address a conflict between management and its employees. Five years earlier, the company had fallen on hard times and was nearly bankrupt. Everyone knew that the company was facing a fragile situation, and the employees were concerned not only for the viability of the company, but also for their jobs. Many of the employees had worked for the organization for decades and felt a tremendous loyalty to it. In a move of desperation, the management team asked its employees to help them avoid bankruptcy by taking pay cuts. They asked everyone to "pull together and win together." All agreed, and the company hobbled along for the next five years, avoiding the worst-case scenario.

Unexpectedly, the company started doing very well again, and it was clear that the "pull together and win together" strategy had worked. But this is where the trouble began. The employees fully expected that when the company started doing well again, their pay would be restored. This did not happen. Moreover, the management team gave themselves big bonuses, arguing that it was a legitimate move and was in their contract. From the executives' point of view, they did nothing wrong.

The outcry from the employees was immediate. They felt betrayed. What happened to "pull together and win together"? They had given the leaders the benefit of the doubt, believing that if the company ever started doing better, they would do the right thing. The trust that the employees had felt for the management team during the crisis vanished. The workers felt exploited and violated in so many ways that it led to a complete breakdown in the relationship with the management team.

In addition to the betrayal of trust, the employees felt that their dignity had been violated in many ways. They were treated *unfairly*; it felt like a great injustice. They felt invisible— as if their identities didn't matter. They were not being *recognized* or *acknowledged* for the contribution they had made to help the company survive. They no longer felt *safe* in their relationship with management. "There's no telling what they will do to us," one work group reported. They felt *excluded* from the windfall the company experienced, but what bothered the employees the most was that the management didn't want to talk about the bonuses, much less be held *accountable* for their actions. One worker summed it up this way: "Management keeps saying that it was legal to take the bonuses—it was in their contract. *Just because it's legal doesn't mean it's right.*"

You can see how nearly all the elements of dignity were compromised in one decision by the management team. The team's silence and unwillingness to have a dialogue only made it worse. What were the chances that trust could be restored? Unfortunately, the executives were not willing to take any responsibility for their decision, which made it impossible for the relationships to be repaired. The company never recovered from the rift with its employees.

Manuel Guillén and Tomás González, business professors at the University of Valencia in Spain, explain that people expect their leaders and managers to behave morally.[4] To maintain a good relationship with their followers, leaders need not only to be technically good at what they do, but also to demonstrate a commitment to do what is right for others. They say that leadership has an ethical dimension related to treating others well—to honoring their dignity. This ethical dimension is present when the relationship between leaders and those who follow them is the strongest and trust is at its highest. By contrast, trust is quickly lost when leaders stray from doing what is right.

The human reaction to a breakdown in trust is swift and automatic. It is part of our evolutionary legacy, passed down to us like a dominant gene. We are very quick to exclude others from our moral circle when we feel betrayed, especially by people we felt connected to and empathic toward.[5] One neuroscientist explains that empathy and disgust are mediated in part by the same brain region.[6] It makes sense, then, that a breakdown in a high level of empathy can elicit a very strong reaction of disgust. In the earlier story, the breakdown of trust and empathy was just one dignity violation away, and it was safe to say that when that violation happened, the employees were left with a feeling of disgust.

Paul Zak, a professor of economics, management, and psychology at Claremont Graduate University, has studied trust and written extensively about the role it plays in creating a productive work environment.[7] In an article he wrote for the *Harvard Business Review*, he reported that trust is good for business.[8] Creating a culture of trust in an organization increases productivity, cooperation, discretionary energy, and employee retention. People report feeling happier and supported in an environment where stronger performance is nurtured.

One of the findings of his research is that when people feel trust in someone, a brain chemical called oxytocin is produced. This chemical signals that a person is safe to approach. His research indicates that the more people trust others, the more their brains produce oxytocin. In another series of studies, he administered oxytocin (through a nasal spray) in subjects and found that those who were given the spray were twice as likely to act trusting toward a stranger as those who did not receive it. He also found that stress worked against trusting others. Finally, he reported that oxytocin increases empathy.

After conducting a series of experiments inside companies, Zak has come up with eight management behaviors that nurture trust:

- *Recognize excellence.* When an employee accomplishes a goal, give public recognition.
- *Induce challenge stress.* Encourage the team to take on a job that requires hard work, is somewhat stressful, but is attainable. The brains of the team members will release oxytocin, strengthening the bond among them.
- *Give people discretion in how they work.* People react positively to being trusted to do the job in their own way. Autonomy promotes innovation.
- *Enable job crafting.* To the extent possible, let people choose to do the work they feel most passionate about.
- *Share information broadly.* When people feel they know the direction in which the company is going, they feel less stress.

Uncertainty surrounding the goals and aspirations of an organization creates stress for the workers—and this in turn
inhibits the production of oxytocin, which reduces team co-
hesion.

- *Intentionally build relationships.* When people are encouraged to develop good relationships at work, their performance improves.
- *Facilitate whole-person growth.* Workplaces that support and
encourage the ongoing growth and development of their
employees, both personally and professionally, promote a
culture of trust.
- *Show your own vulnerability.* When leaders recognize their
limits and ask their employees for help, oxytocin is stimu-
lated, increasing the workers' trust and desire to cooperate.
Significantly, asking for help is perceived not as a sign of
weakness but as demonstrating a commitment to continued
learning and growth.

Looking at Zak's findings from a dignity perspective,
there are significant parallels. It appears that many of the things
that leaders can do to promote dignity will promote trust in
work relationships, in part through promoting the production
of oxytocin. These factors include recognizing workers for a
job well done, allowing them control and independence in
how they achieve their work goals, making it safe to be emotionally vulnerable, nurturing an environment that facilitates
ongoing growth and development, trusting that employees can
contribute to the company when they are doing the work they
feel passionate about, and encouraging relationship-building
as a company goal. After all, dignity resides and flourishes in
strong, mutually enhancing relationships.

It is obvious that consciously promoting trust in organizations is good for business. Zak's research findings demonstrate that employees who work in high-trust companies feel more engaged, more energetic, more loyal, and more likely to stay with their employer, and they tended to recommend the company to others. People also reported enjoying their jobs, feeling aligned with their purpose, and experiencing good relationships with their colleagues. In short, high-trust companies provide opportunities to improve how employees treat one another. I think it's safe to say that these cultures promote dignity as well as empathy.

Trust and vulnerability are both dimensions and manifestations of dignity consciousness. In reality, they are intertwined and interdependent, but they require a separate and careful look in order to understand the profound effects they have on each other and our well-being.

9
Activate Empathy

Self-absorption in all its forms kills empathy, let alone compassion. When we focus on ourselves, our world contracts as our problems and preoccupations loom large. But when we focus on others, our world expands. Our own problems drift to the periphery of the mind and so seem smaller, and we increase our capacity for connection—or compassionate action.

                                        —Daniel Goleman

There has been a lot of interest in the concept of empathy and the role it plays in our lives and relationships. In his book *Social Intelligence: The New Science of Human Relationships*, Daniel Goleman explains that one of the most gratifying human experiences is "the experience of being experienced," or what he calls mutual empathy.[1]

   He also tells us what we already know from an earlier chapter about our shared human experience—that we are wired to connect with others. The research shows that, because we are wired to connect, we are also keenly set to read the intentions of others and to empathize. Goleman defines empathy in three ways: *knowing* (cognitively understanding) what others are feeling; *feeling* (experiencing) what others are feeling; and *responding compassionately* (acting) to another's distress. He sums it up this way: "I notice you, I feel with you, and so I act to help you."[2]

What is remarkable about empathy is that, when we empathize with another, the brain activates the same neural pathway in each of us. Goleman explains, "In other words, to understand what someone else experiences—to empathize— we utilize the same brain wiring that is active during our own experience. Our mirror neurons are in synch, allowing us to communicate without words. What's on their mind occupies ours."[3]

He makes the point throughout that without empathy, relationships suffer. Empathy inhibits cruelty toward others. It has the power to silence the amygdala, the part of the brain that can trigger aggressive behavior. Without our capacity for empathy, the human experience of relationship would not be a natural source of comfort and safety, but potentially a source of threat and harm.

Maia Szalavitz and Bruce Perry, authors of *Born for Love: Why Empathy Is Essential—and Endangered,* argue that empathy is at the core of our capacity to love. "We survive because we can love. And we love because we can empathize—that is, stand in another's shoes and care about what it feels like to be there."[4] Empathizing with others is experiencing their situation, not yours. Szalavitz and Perry advise us that empathy lies at the heart of everything that makes human relationships work—trust, collaboration, and caring for others. They blame a failure to empathize on many social ills such as racism, conflict, and violence of all kinds.

Even though we are all born for love and empathy—we have the biological predisposition wired into our brains—there is no guarantee that we will develop it. Szalavitz and Perry tell us that the gifts of our biology give us only the potential for empathy. Infants need the experience of love and attention to activate the capacity for empathy, and then they (and we) need it for the rest of our lives. Empathy requires lifelong caring and loving interactions with others. Here is where I find the connection between empathy and dignity, for what a powerful demonstration of love and caring it is to honor each other's dignity.

Goleman, Szalavitz, and Perry all paint a positive picture about empathy, but not all empathy experts do. I'd like to describe some other recent research that has questioned, and sparked a debate about, the unequivocal value of empathy.

In his book *Against Empathy: The Case for Rational Compassion,* Yale psychologist Paul Bloom looks at the darker side of empathy.[5] He makes a distinction between emotional and cognitive empathy; emotional empathy requires one to match the feeling of the other person, whereas cognitive empathy requires only an understanding of the feeling; you don't have to experience someone's pain to understand that someone is in pain.

According to Bloom, in making a decision about the right thing to do, it is actually dangerous to depend on emotional empathy because there are biases embedded in it. We can empathize more with people who are like us—those for whom we have a natural bias to care for and protect. This "spotlighting" of the targets of our empathy (toward only those we care about and who are like us) demonstrates the limits of the primal emotion: our implicit biases enable us to empathize with some but not all human beings. He thinks that if we are trying to make a decision about how we should act, it is better to go with cognitive empathy, sidestepping the emotional bias. Using a "cognitive," cost-benefit analysis is more effective when trying to do the right thing. In his words, "I want to make the case for the value of conscious, deliberative reasoning in everyday life, arguing that we should strive to use our heads rather than our hearts."[6] Bloom has called the emotional aspect of empathy innumerate and biased. "We are not psychologically constituted to feel toward a stranger as we feel toward someone we love."[7] He argues that we should try to treat everyone as we would those we love, but this requires a conscious decision on our part with a commitment to establishing equal and just treatment for all. We can't rely on emotional empathy for that. Would honoring the dignity of everyone we come in contact with fulfill that commitment?

In an op-ed piece in the *New York Times* entitled "Empathy Is Actually a Choice," authors Darly Cameron, Michael Inzlicht, and William A. Cunningham agree that empathy is not always the feeling that animates us to do the right thing.[8] They too warn us that it isn't that simple. Their research has shown that there are circumstances that mitigate our use of empathy as a motivation to act morally. They explain that the limits to our ability to empathize often depend on how we *want* to feel. It appears that we can turn our capacity for empathy on or off, depending on when we *choose* to do so. They cite other research that shows that empathy can not only be turned on and off but also can be improved, defying the traditional notion that it is a fixed trait.[9]

Another disturbing finding that these authors reported was that powerful people tend to empathize less. Even peo-

ple who were arbitrarily assigned powerful roles showed a de-
crease in empathy. Their explanation? "People with a higher
sense of power exhibit less empathy because they have less incentive to interact with others."

In *Behave: The Biology of Humans at Our Best and Worst*,
Robert Sapolsky reports research findings that reveal how,
across the socioeconomic spectrum, the wealthier people are,
the less likely they are to show empathy for people in distress
and the less likely they are to act compassionately.[10]

What are the implications of this critique of empathy for
those who want to lead with dignity? When fostering meaningful connections with others, especially those who have en-
trusted us to act on their behalf, it is essential to empathize with
them for the connection to be authentic. I'm not convinced that
leaders have to *feel with others* (emotional empathy); understanding what others are feeling (cognitive empathy) is probably
enough to communicate caring and concern. The explanation
that people with power exhibit less empathy because they have
less incentive to interact with others is a violation of the basic
premise on which leading with dignity is built. The three connections I described earlier that are at the heart of a dignified
life (connection to your own dignity, to the dignity of others,
and to the dignity of something greater than yourself) mean
that interacting with others in ways that honor their value and
worth is at the heart of dignified behavior. Choosing not to
interact with or to show little empathy toward others in the
organization is a failure of leadership. It's impossible to lead
with dignity without human connection.

In Chapter 8, I described a company that was on the
verge of bankruptcy. In a desperate moment, the management
team asked its employees to take pay cuts to avoid the collapse
of the company. The loyal employees trusted the team's judg-

ment and decided to get on board with the "pull together and win together" policy. Everyone was feeling the same pain—the empathy factor ran high during those trying times.

When the executive management team decided to take bonuses but not restore the employees' pay, it is safe to say that the executives *chose* to turn off their empathy for the employees. Beyond their lament that it was legal for them to take the bonuses, the managers were silent about their decision. They chose not to interact with the employees about it—there was no engagement or willingness to empathically hear and discuss their grievances. Did the executives' positions of power disable their natural empathy?

Frans de Waal, author of *The Age of Empathy*, agrees that we are born with the natural desire to be in relationship with others.[11] (As I reported earlier, we have evolved the need for connections with others to ensure our survival; there was safety in numbers.[12]) De Waal tells us that the ability to empathize is the glue that connects people. Being able to feel what others experience enables us to care for them, ensuring lasting bonds.

He also points out that when we are treated with hostility (when our dignity is violated), the relationship is the first thing to go. Instead of feeling empathic toward the offender, our old brain (amygdala) triggers a powerful automatic reaction to disconnect—to fight or flee. Empathy is the greatest casualty of conflict. Without empathy, it is difficult to maintain the three humanizing connections (to self, other, and the world). All we care about is eliminating the source of the threat. Our need for self-preservation overrides our need for connection.

Consider the example in Chapter 8 where the employees expressed their outrage and feelings of betrayal toward the management team about their bonuses. Given what we've learned, it should come as no surprise that their relationship broke down along with their capacity for empathy. From a dignity perspective, the threat experienced by both the management team and the employees destroyed the trust that was the foundation of the relationship during the "pull together and win together" stage. To avoid the shame of being exposed for a wrongdoing—that is, to save face—the management team might have been tempted to avoid taking responsibility for contributing to the breakdown of the relationship. Without the "primal" or "emotional empathy" that had held them together during the difficult times, all kinds of violating behaviors dominated the interactions between the executives and workers.

Whatever role empathy plays in doing the right thing—it may be complicated and has its limits—to argue "against empathy" seems extreme. As Goleman said, one of the most gratifying human experiences is to "experience being experienced." Whether we choose to emotionally empathize with someone or it occurs spontaneously, the result is a connection between people. Bloom invites us to use reason and cost-benefit analyses in deciding how we are going to act toward others. But even if using cold, calculating, unemotional decisions will correctly determine what is just and moral, if you want to demonstrate to people that you care about them and value them, you need more than that. If you recognize that they matter (honor their dignity) and respond to how they are feeling (empathize), you will go far beyond doing what is right to doing what we have come into the world equipped to seek: *meaningful human connection.*

Here are some reflections about empathy that could help us establish and maintain dignified connections with others:

- *In your interactions with others, be aware of when you experience empathy and when you do not.* Know the difference. When you do not feel natural empathy toward people, it could set you up for violating their dignity, knowingly or unknowingly.
- *Recognize that even if you don't feel natural empathy for others, you can still choose to honor their dignity.* You do not have to feel emotional empathy to treat people well.
- *We can improve and activate our natural inclination for empathy by treating others with dignity.* Doing so can set off a chain of dignity-honoring exchanges that could ultimately end in a genuine, felt connection, even among groups for whom mutual empathy does not come easily.

The quotation by Goleman that opens this chapter warns us that self-absorption kills empathy. If we want to lead with dignity, it is important that we divide our attention between our world within and the world outside of us. Too much focus on our inner worlds takes us away from noticing and reacting to what is happening in the world around us. What we should consider adopting is what Ronald Heifetz calls the balcony perspective, that is, taking a bird's-eye view of our behavior while in the midst of fast-paced interactions with others.

10

Head to the Balcony

Few practical ideas are more obvious or more critical than the need to get perspective in the midst of action.
—Ronald Heifetz

One of the essential skills for leading with dignity is being able to see yourself from a perspective beyond your own. Ron Heifetz, a leadership expert at Harvard's Kennedy School of Government, describes the importance of being able to "go to the balcony" to get a broader perspective on what is happening in the midst of action.[1] He explains that, by mentally stepping up to the balcony while embroiled in intense interactions with others, one is able to answer the questions, "What's really going on here? What role am I playing in this drama? Are there bigger forces at work that are contributing to this failed interaction?" This mental exercise helps us gain a broader perspective when we might otherwise get caught up in the ten temptations—among other self-destructive behaviors. Pushing the pause button and reflecting on our behavior could prevent dignity violations to others and ourselves.

But getting to the balcony isn't easy, especially when we are emotionally hijacked during heated discussions.[2] When our vengeful "Me" takes over our thinking and actions, we are likely to regret our behavior. Our self-preservation instincts are set for our individual protection, not for protecting our relationships.

For example, I once worked with a woman who was having a difficult time in her staff meetings. She found that there were circumstances when one or more of the people in her charge would make what she felt were provocative statements about her, and she would respond by taking the bait: she would lash back at them, often returning the harm, violating their dignity as well as her own. The discussion would become so emotionally charged that she would have to simply end the meetings.

When I told her about the balcony metaphor—how she could mentally push the pause button and head to a metaphorical balcony before responding to the provocative statements—she was eager to learn how to do it. I explained to her that, while she was on the balcony, she could gain a momentary perspective on what was happening in the meetings, enabling her to see the bigger picture of what she looked like in her interactions with her staff. What was happening to her in those moments when she felt the need to lash back? What was being triggered inside of her that gave rise to her inability to hold back and not take the bait?

Getting on the balcony can help us see two dynamics that are at play and likely contributing to the problem: first, what's happening in our "world within," and second, what is happening in the outside world. It enables us to zoom in and out of being in the interaction and thus to gain some distance from it.

Starting with the world within, we can ask ourselves, "What just happened to me?" Observing ourselves engaging with others is a sophisticated cognitive skill that requires us to hold our threatened and emotionally triggered selves in check before we violate the dignity of others, as well as our own. We do not look good when we take the bait. Even though it feels like we have a right to defend ourselves or to get even, that kind of thinking comes from our self-preservation instincts, not from thoughtful self-reflection. We are acting from the automatic, impulsive reaction of our "Me," not our more grounded and expansive "I" perspective.

Here's an interesting side note to what happens to us when we are emotionally hijacked. Neuroscientist Jill Bolte Taylor describes the limbic system—the part of our brain that is responsible for our emotional reactions—as not maturing as we go through our lifetimes. Unlike our neocortex, the "emotional brain" that we inherit when we are born never grows or develops. What is blank at birth is the neocortex, not our emotional brain. She explains: "When our emotional buttons are pushed, we retain the ability to react to incoming stimulation as though we were a two-year-old, even when we are adults."[3] How many times have you observed yourself or others reacting like a two-year-old when emotionally hijacked by an encounter with another person?

Yet we are not doomed to react in childlike ways when we experience a threat from someone. She notes that we also have the capacity, with the help of the neocortex, to manage these highly charged emotional reactions and behave in more mature, thoughtful ways.

When we enter into leadership positions, we bring along

with us a powerful history concerning our own dignity. Whether we are conscious of it or not, our early experiences of having our dignity violated, if left unaddressed and unhealed, can have a lasting effect on the health of our inner worlds as adults.[4] For example, if our early relationships in our formative years were fraught with dignity violations such as being provoked or criticized by someone on a routine basis, being treated in a similar way as an adult could trigger a strong response—often a stronger response than the situation calls for.

Going to the balcony when the feeling first arises can help us to recognize that our response is being influenced by what I call an *early imprint to our dignity* that has not been adequately understood and addressed from an adult perspective. The helpless feelings all of us had when our dignity was violated as children, when we are truly dependent on our caretakers, can be at the core of our triggered reactions to similar interactions we have as adults.[5] Understanding our dignity vulnerabilities, which stem from those early experiences of being treated as less than worthy, can make it easier to resist the temptations to lash back at others (to "take the bait"). With the help of the metaphorical balcony, we can see that our reactions may be the result of an outdated, childlike framing of who we are and what happened to us. Being aware of our dignity sensitivities, doing what I call a vulnerability inventory, can help us push the pause button when those sensitivities are triggered by people around us.

What is a vulnerability inventory? Using the ten essential elements of dignity as a guide, consider which of these elements were violated early on in your life. Did you often feel that you were discriminated against because of something about your identity that you could do nothing about (perhaps your race, class, religion, sex, or ethnic group)? Did you routinely feel psychologically or physically unsafe in your home or at school (were you mistreated or abused either emotionally or physically)? Were you treated as invisible by a parent or others who were responsible for you? Taking the other elements one by one, ask yourself how often you experienced violations to your dignity and what the circumstances were.

With this exercise, it doesn't take long to figure out where your dignity vulnerabilities are. Not only can you can recapture a mental picture of what you experienced by using the elements as a guide, but you can also see the connection between your early mistreatment and how similar events in the present can trigger the old painful injuries to your dignity.

What is critical to understand about your *early imprints of indignity* is that, at least for certain situations, they have frozen you into "Me" consciousness, where you believe that your dignity is based on the way others treat you. These imprints also set you up for the temptation to lash back or fall prey to any of the other ten temptations. The default reaction is an automatic defense response, in which you guard your already wounded dignity with a vengeance. Under these circumstances, all your "Me" wants to do is eliminate the source of the threat—that is, to psychologically (or even, in extreme cases, physically) annihilate the person who triggered the old injury.

Richard Davidson, an affective neuroscientist and professor at the University of Wisconsin, Madison, explains that although our emotional "style" and reactions can be set early in our lives, we also have what it takes to change them.[6] As adults, we can train ourselves to alter the response patterns in our brains. He explains that there has been a revolution in our understanding of neuroplasticity. Scientists used to think that the brain doesn't change. But breakthroughs in neuroscience have shown us that our brains can change as a result of purely mental activity (thoughts and intentions). Davidson is a proponent of meditation to quiet the brain during emotional turmoil. Mindfulness meditation—observing our thoughts in a nonjudgmental way—can help us regain control of otherwise out-of-control thoughts and behaviors.

Kevin Ochsner's work on cognitive reframing confirms that thinking differently about an event can change our emotional experience of it.[7]

The capacity to lead with dignity is strongly enhanced by understanding the role the balcony perspective could play in gaining deeper and broader insights about ourselves during emotionally charged interactions with others. This perspective enables us to

- Recognize and intercept automatic, self-preservation behaviors that are triggered under these circumstances.
- Identify, with the use of the vulnerability inventory, injuries to our dignity that occurred early in life and have left us hypersensitive to similar experiences as adults.
- Reframe the interaction from a "Me" perspective to an "I" outlook, which allows for a broader understanding of what is happening, including not only our reactions but also other points of view.

As I pointed out earlier, the balcony perspective helps us examine two dynamics that are at play during challenging interactions with others: what is happening in our world and what might be happening on the outside, from the perspective of those with whom we are interacting. Without the emotional upheaval inside us, we can take the time to imagine what we might be missing about what is happening to those with whom we are engaged. We can ask ourselves, "Am I assuming I'm an innocent victim in this failed relationship?" "Could I have unknowingly done something that violated this person's dignity?" "Do I have a full understanding of his or her point of view?" "Am I missing information that could explain his or her provocative behavior?" "Is this person missing information that could explain the gaps in their awareness of what I am up against, of the forces that are influencing me?"

Let's return to the story of the woman (I will call her Amy) who had such difficulty in her staff meetings. Learning about the balcony and discussing her dignity vulnerabilities has made a big difference in the way in which she interacts with her employees in her weekly meetings.

Using the vulnerability inventory, she became aware of how significant violations to her dignity, early in her life, left an imprint on how she felt about herself in the present, which in turn caused her to react strongly to even a hint of criticism from her direct reports. She explained that her mother, a perfectionist, criticized her for every little thing. She could not tolerate it when Amy made mistakes or didn't perform up to her high standards. Moreover, when Amy went to kindergarten, she had a teacher who was just like her mother. The anxiety that Amy felt about not being perfect created so much tension within her that whenever her mother or the teacher pointed out her flaws, she would end up feeling unworthy; their criticism triggered a sense of deep shame and incompetence.

Amy did have an awareness of the extent to which her mother's criticism of her affected the way she felt about herself. She had spent some time in therapy and recognized the impact of her relationship with her mother. What was new and different for her was the act of dignity framing—of recognizing how her early wounds from childhood were affecting her leadership abilities. Her inclination was to control everything in the staff meetings so that no one would be able to say anything negative about her. When they did, she would get very upset with those who spoke up, violating their dignity in the process. The environment would quickly become toxic to both Amy and her staff.

The balcony perspective is a technique for creating the space we need to ponder the complexities of both our worlds within and the worlds of others outside of us. Creating space for reflection before falling prey to the ten temptations gives us time to think about which part of ourselves we want to be in charge of our decision making: do we want our reactive and vengeful "Me" calling the shots, or our reflective, caring, responsible, dignity-conscious "I"? And what is the next step after our trip to the balcony? What do we do when we realize that we might have contributed to the breakdown in the relationship? (Hint: It involves more climbing!)

11

Take Responsibility

The price of greatness is responsibility.
—*Winston Churchill*

lizabeth Samet, author of *Leadership: Essential Writings by Our Greatest Thinkers,* opens her chapter "Taking Responsibility" with the following quotation by Abraham Lincoln: "I now wish to make the personal acknowledgment that you were right, and I was wrong" (from a letter to Ulysses S. Grant, July 13, 1863).[1] President Lincoln was apologizing for expressing doubts about General Grant's strategy leading up to the Union army's victory in Vicksburg.

Samet comments that, as President Lincoln demonstrated, it takes great courage to admit to being wrong. Certainly, courage is important, but I think it takes more than that. If we think about what courage is—the ability to do something that frightens us—then what is it that we fear when we admit to being wrong or own up to a mistake?[2] Why is courage even necessary?

From a dignity perspective, what we fear is looking bad in the eyes of others; we worry that our sense of worth is on the line. The drive to avoid losing face is so strong that it provokes good people to cover up and lie to prevent the truth from ruining their status and image.[3] The pull of the ten temptations is so powerful that the instinct to hide the truth about what we have done feels automatic when the fear of being exposed is imminent. For someone who is in the dependent stage of dignity awareness and who believes that her dignity comes from others' approval and praise, the fear of a loss of dignity and the shame that accompanies it can compound the issue, making the situation truly debilitating.

The capacity to take responsibility for our actions rests on a foundation of knowledge about the human experience. We are continually being challenged by our evolutionary legacy and the instincts that we all have for self-preservation (the ten temptations to violate dignity). Without knowledge of these mental processes that are triggered under circumstances of threat (to our worth, status, and our image in the eyes of others), we are likely to get lured into destructive behaviors when we are faced with our own wrongdoing, mistake, or something else that may make us appear weak and incompetent. The temptation to cover up what we have done is so strong that even with awareness of the gravitational pull of these survival instincts, it is still difficult to overcome.

Along with courage, taking responsibility for your actions requires being grounded in the knowledge of your worth. It means being connected to your own dignity and knowing that no matter what you do, right or wrong, your dignity is still intact. It's the only antidote that is strong enough to stand up to our inherent fear of humiliation and public exposure.[4]

Fears of humiliation and loss of status are formidable internal foes, and yes, we need courage to stand up to them.[5] But we also need a commitment to defend and protect our dignity and the dignity of those who would be harmed by our lies and deceit. This is where truth and vulnerability converge. Taking responsibility for our actions, no matter how shameful, requires us to face the truth of both our inherent value as well as our vulnerability to the ten temptations. Will we take the bait and lash back instead of taking seriously the perspective of others? Will we face the truth and own up to our mistake or wrongdoing? Will we shirk responsibility or blame and shame others to deflect our guilt? Will we resist the feedback from others that can help us see our blind spots—the very gaps that probably contributed to our making the mistake to begin with?

Let's revisit the situation I introduced in Chapter 10 involving Amy and her leadership challenges during her staff meetings. Amy learned how to mentally take herself out of the moment when she felt herself reacting to the provocative statements from her staff. Employing the "balcony perspective," whereby she could observe herself and her responses to the emotionally charged interchanges with her direct reports, enabled her to see how she was contributing to the problem by taking the bait when she felt criticized.

The balcony perspective also allowed her to see how she was reacting from early wounds to her dignity, which were influencing her behavior in the present. The vulnerability inventory helped her identify the early imprints of indignity that were making her hypersensitive to criticism. From the balcony, she was able to stop herself from escalating the negative interactions with her staff. She was also able to engage her "I" consciousness, to see how she could respond in a way that preserved not only her staff's dignity, but also her own. The next step for Amy was to meet with her staff and take responsibility for the part she had played in their history of failed interactions.

Even though Amy had a good understanding of why she reacted the way she did when she perceived criticism from her staff, and she was confident that the balcony perspective would help her, she was still fighting the temptation to save face. There remained a part of her that was afraid that her direct reports would lose respect for her and would perceive her as incompetent. Her fear of being judged was as strong as her fear of humiliation.

One thing to remember about initiating a behavior change such as the one Amy was aspiring to do is that the fear of humiliation does not go away overnight. She needed to shift her understanding of where her own dignity came from—to move beyond the dependent stage in which she believed her sense of worth relied on the way others saw her and treated her. Helping her see that her dignity was inherent and unconditional, that it was in her hands, and that no one could take it away from her took time. With a lot of coaching and help from her loved ones and therapist, she finally achieved Mandela consciousness. She was ready to start taking responsibility.

One advantage Amy had going into her meeting with her direct reports was that I had met with them several times, preparing them for what Amy was about to do—take responsibility for the way she treated them in the dreaded staff meetings. I explained that they would have an opportunity to give Amy feedback about the dignity violations they experienced from her during the meetings. I also explained how important it was to give her the feedback in a way she could hear it. Screaming and yelling at her would not work. I learned from Thomas Scheff and Suzanne Retzinger, authors of *Emotions and Violence: Shame and Rage in Destructive Conflicts,* that a small amount of feeling shamed or embarrassed by what we have done is a good motivator of change.[6] If, however, the shame reaches an intolerable level, brought on by strong emotional attacks, it is much harder to fight our self-preservation instincts; instead we tend to succumb to the ten temptations.

When Amy finally met with her staff, I was there to facilitate the encounter. Amy began by saying that her relationship with them was very important to her and that she wanted to do whatever she could to repair the damage done by past violations of their dignity that she had committed. She explained that she was unaware of the extent to which she had impulsively reacted to their attempts at feedback in the past, shutting them down and failing to acknowledge their concerns. She said that the dignity training she received had helped her see her blind spots, and she wanted to apologize for the harm she had done to them and to their relationship. She wanted to hear their feedback, not just during this session, but on a regular basis. She told them she wanted to make it a normal part of their staff meetings. If something was bothering them, she wanted to know about it. She also acknowledged how difficult it must have been for them to not feel safe to speak up when something didn't feel right.

Amy invited the staff to give her feedback, which they had practiced during my session with them. She was instructed to "listen to understand," and the staff was instructed to "speak to be understood." Amy was also instructed to listen for the dignity violations in their stories and feedback. She knew that she was not allowed to speak or defend herself while they were talking. Her job was to listen as carefully as she could to achieve a deeper understanding of the negative impact she had had on them. Taking responsibility first meant opening herself up to hearing their stories.

Amy listened with compassion and concern for what she had put her staff through. When they had finished giving her feedback, she took the appropriate next step—she apologized and acknowledged how hard it must have been for them. She ended by restating that she was committed to being open in the future to their feedback, making it a normal part of how they interact with her.

The outcome of the encounter with Amy's staff was not what she had expected. She was sure that, having destroyed the trust of her employees by repeatedly violating their dignity (although unknowingly), reconciling with them would take considerable time, with Amy slowly regaining this lost trust. But something remarkable happened when she made herself vulnerable with them. By accepting responsibility for the harm she had done and then apologizing for violating their dignity, she made it possible for them to empathize with her. They were familiar with the ten temptations from a training session I had done with them, and they recognized the courage it took for her to do what she did. They could see the strength and vulnerability that it took for her to risk more judgment from them, and they were moved by her willingness to face her truth.

Amy's staff not only accepted her apology, but many also felt inspired by her sincere desire to right the wrongs in their relationship. One of them told me after the meeting, "If Amy can take responsibility for her actions, it gives me hope that if I were in the same situation, I could do it, too." When Amy admitted her guilt and took responsibility for her role in the problem, it not only repaired the relationship, but also made it stronger than it had ever been. The level of intimacy that developed in which the coworkers felt free to speak up and be their authentic selves in the relationship surprised everyone.

The reconciliation had other effects as well. Amy and the

staff worked much better as a team, and the increase in the level of productivity that resulted was significant. They also reported feeling more engaged in their work and proud of the contributions they were making to the company.

Amy's story is a perfect example of how taking responsibility for one's actions affects all three dignity connections (the three Cs): the connection to your own dignity, the connection to the dignity of others, and finally, the connection to the dignity of something greater than yourself. In this case, the third C was Amy's connection to the dignity of the company. The distraction that Amy's failed leadership had created in her team had impaired her ability to do her job—to serve in her role and contribute to the company. After taking responsibility for her leadership mistakes, she was able to see how out of alignment she was in all three dignity connections. She experienced firsthand not only the effects of being disconnected from dignity and the suffering this disconnection creates, but also the transformative power of reconnection, when all three dimensions of dignity are in alignment. She discovered that taking responsibility was not just about her and her individual actions. She became aware of the interconnection among her dignity, the dignity of others, and the greater purpose they were all serving as employees of the company. Just as dignity is about the three Cs, it also requires responsibility, responsibility, and responsibility.

Most important, she learned that learning about dignity was much bigger than understanding her value and worth. How she felt about her own dignity affected how she treated others and affected everyone's capacity, including her own, to work toward a common purpose. As Davie Floyd reminded us, and as Amy's experience demonstrated, we are all responsible for dignity. It's our duty to protect and nurture it, in all its incarnations.

Here are some important things to remember (about what it means to be human) that make it challenging to take responsibility:

- *Taking responsibility does not come naturally.* We are all up against the same human struggle—coming clean when we have done something wrong. If we're having trouble admitting to a wrongdoing, that should not come as a surprise. We need dignity consciousness to fight the fear of humiliation and the powerful temptation to save face.
- *Without Mandela consciousness, it is more difficult to overcome our resistance to taking responsibility.* Knowing that no one can take away your dignity—that it is ultimately in your hands only—provides the emotional stability that enables us to take responsibility for things we do.
- *Like any other kind of learning, taking responsibility requires effort and practice.* Start practicing owning up to mistakes with trusted friends and loved ones. Know that when you take responsibility for your actions, you are maintaining and protecting your own dignity—remembering this helps temper the fear of humiliation and keeps the ten temptations at bay.

The principles I have introduced in Part 2 illustrate how all of the capacities and behaviors that I have highlighted in this section are interrelated. Leading with *dignity consciousness* enables us to see our responsibility to care for and protect our inherent value and worth as well as that of others for the greater good. Awareness of the three Cs guides our actions, forcing us to be more humble and less focused on protecting and caring for just our own well-being.

This expanded view of human responsibility provides us with a check on our all-too-common tendency to think and act as if the boundaries of our concerns begin and end with ourselves. The humility that is required to see ourselves as part of the whole, instead of the whole itself, frees us from the shackles of arrogance, narcissism, and narrow self-interest. Being part of the whole means that *everyone matters*. We are important, but so is everyone else. Exercising dignified leadership means embodying the humility that comes from this expanded *dignity consciousness*.

It takes a humble, responsible leader to not only create safe environments where people can be vulnerable, but also cultivate trust, recognize the need to "head to the balcony," act in ways that show a lifelong commitment to learning, show empathy, and take responsibility for the harm that he or she has caused others. As leaders, we need to be open to change, to be aware that we may not always be right, and to recognize that we need feedback from others to illuminate our blind spots— to help us see what we cannot see. Humility will keep us from falling into the far too common narcissistic trap that makes us think that when push comes to shove, we know better.

III
Creating a Culture of Dignity

Culture eats strategy for breakfast.
—*Peter Drucker*

12

Advocate for Dignity Education

Is it possible to reinvent organizations, to devise a new model that makes work productive, fulfilling, and meaningful? Can we create soulful workplaces—schools, hospitals, businesses, and nonprofits—where our talents can blossom and our callings can be honored?

—*Frederic Laloux*

U p to this point, I have been focusing on the interpersonal and relational skills and competencies necessary to lead with dignity. When I first visited organizations as a consultant using the Dignity Model, I would begin by identifying the interpersonal violations at the root of the conflicts, using the model to name the wounds and repair the relationships. It didn't take long for me to see that I was missing other forces that were acting on the parties.

I made some mistakes in those early days. Not that the

Dignity Model wasn't relevant. It was. But I needed to step up on the balcony to get a broader perspective on what else was contributing to the conflicts. The mistakes I had made were about the larger context in which the relationship problems were occurring.

What I learned was that it wasn't enough to introduce the basic building blocks of the model to the specific people who were experiencing the conflict and expect that everything would be fine. I learned that without a *systemwide* understanding of dignity and the role it plays in our lives and relationships—without everyone in the organization on board—dysfunctional aspects of the *broader culture* would influence the target groups with which I was working.

It was often the case that the organization's culture itself created violations of dignity. Unspoken and unaddressed norms of acceptable treatment determined the way in which people interacted, and ignorance of all things related to dignity was ubiquitous. Because leaders lacked an understanding of how vulnerable people are to having their dignity violated, they were not mindful of how some of their decisions were affecting the morale of the entire workforce.

I'd like to go back to a story I told in Chapter 8 about an organization that was on the verge of bankruptcy and that asked its employees to take pay cuts to avoid the demise of the company. When the crisis was over, the executives' decision to take bonuses instead of returning the missed pay to its employees felt, to the workers, like a gross violation of their dignity. The unfairness of the decision, along with the workers' sense of betrayal, created an organization-wide pushback from the employees. This was an example not of an interpersonal failure to honor dignity, but of a *policy decision* that negatively affected all workers and created a toxic work culture.

This experience helped me to see that dignity education requires learning both interpersonal skills (how to interact with others in a way that recognizes their value and worth) as well as systemic applications (how to create policies and procedures that consider the impact on the dignity of everyone in the organization).

By this time, it should come as no surprise that few organizations with which I have worked had been exposed to dignity education or had integrated the knowledge into their policies and procedures. Educating ourselves about the significant role that dignity plays in our lives and how to treat others with full recognition that they matter should be a high priority in our educational system, but it is not. Thus many organizations run the risk of developing a culture that gives rise to a variety of dignity-violating behaviors.

I have given many examples so far of how even people who have good intentions unknowingly violate the dignity of others. Some people are not aware of the power they have to affect others. Others do not understand why a righteous justification to return the harm done to them turns them into perpetrators. The wisdom that comes from dignity consciousness—*do not do unto others the harm they have done unto you*—is sadly not the conventional wisdom upon which organizations are built.

What I have learned from my mistakes is that *to establish an organization-wide culture of dignity, everyone needs to be on board.* Most important, the leadership needs to endorse and support it. There must be the willingness to incorporate and embody a knowledge of dignity into the day-to-day functioning of the organization. Dignity consciousness can then become the emotional scaffolding that protects and supports the inherent value and vulnerability of everyone who works in the organization.

The role that leadership plays in creating this safety net cannot be overstated. Leaders' contributions to creating a culture of dignity set the stage, tone, and expectations for how people are treated in the organization and what is expected from them in return. A culture of dignity cannot happen without a culture of responsibility and accountability. The task of leadership is to demonstrate what it looks like to treat people with dignity, modeling the expectations they have for their team. Modeling how to take responsibility for one's actions is equally as important.

At the same time, exercising dignity leadership is not a one-way street. The employees are also responsible for the well-being of each other and the culture. Everyone makes a commitment to upholding the three connections—to one's own dignity, to the dignity of others, and to the dignity of the organization. Employees are responsible for holding leaders accountable for preserving the three Cs, especially when leaders are operating from a blind spot. It takes courage on the part of the employees, but there is no better way to contribute to the growth and development of a leadership team.[1] The result is a workplace where people feel safe—safe to speak up when something doesn't feel right, to be their authentic selves, to learn from mistakes, and to pursue their personal learning goals and aspirations. The other benefit is that they feel a sense of commitment and belonging to the organization.

More than twenty-five years ago, Marvin Weisbord, the author of *Productive Workplaces: Dignity, Meaning and Community in the Twenty-First Century,* noted that engaging everyone in the organization in a process of change improves the whole system.[2] He tells us that actively involving all employees in upholding the values and principles underlying a company's purpose is more important than worrying about methods and techniques. He also points out that engaging everyone in a process of change promotes dignity, gives people a sense that their jobs are contributing to something meaningful, and appeals to our human desire for community (belonging to something greater than ourselves and being a part of a team working together on common goals).

Without a systemwide commitment to creating a culture of dignity, the prevailing, implicit acceptance of everyday violations to dignity makes it difficult for people to bring their full selves to work. As we learned earlier from the work of Robert Kegan and Lisa Laskow Lahey, most people in organizations are doing second jobs in addition to the one they are being paid for.[3] Their second job is hiding their incompetence, covering up their weaknesses, and trying to look good in the eyes of their managers and coworkers.

The fear of looking bad in the eyes of others is a direct consequence of being ignorant of the essential aspects of dignity. It is an example of false dignity—of believing that your sense of worth and validation comes from external sources. Without Mandela consciousness, one of the building blocks of the Dignity Model, all of us can be lured by the temptation to cover up our perceived inadequacies instead of using a mistake or an awareness of the limits of our understanding as an opportunity to expand who we are and to manifest more of our unlimited potential for growth. As I pointed out earlier, the dread of having a wrongdoing or incompetence painfully exposed can make it difficult to own up to mistakes.[4]

The greatest casualty of a shaming culture is self-worth. For a culture of dignity and responsibility to take hold, coming face to face with the debilitating effects of shame and humiliation is the first order of business. The best—and in my experience, the only—way to do this is to help people take ownership of their dignity by encouraging them to develop Mandela consciousness. When we know that our dignity is ours alone, and that it will always remain intact, especially when we make mistakes or reach the limits of what we know, it is much easier to tolerate the discomfort of difficult feedback. As Carol Dweck points out, reaching our limits simply means that we have arrived at a new growth opportunity.[5] There should be no shame in reaching that boundary. Dignity education gives leaders the awareness, knowledge, and skills to replace a culture of shaming with a culture that nurtures people's inherent value and worth, potential for growth, and ability to overcome the all-too-common instinct to cover up a wrongdoing. The fear of being shamed and exposed as inadequate requires a powerful counteracting force. Dignity education is that force.

The dual nature of a culture of dignity, in which people abide by explicit expectations that they will be treated with dignity, and a culture of responsibility, in which everyone is responsible for maintaining their own dignity, the dignity of others, and the dignity of the organization, creates the emotional safety net necessary to keep everyone from being lured by the ten temptations. The stabilizing power of intact dignity trumps the compulsion for self-preservation, especially when the self we are preserving is in desperate need of change.

Frederic Laloux, author of *Reinventing Organizations,* says that to change the nature of an organization, the organization needs a shift in consciousness.[6] He describes a stage model of human consciousness, which begins with the most primitive, egocentric, childlike understanding of the self and the world and ends with a level of consciousness that is inclusive, more complex, and recognizes the interconnectedness of humanity. Similar to Robert Kegan's findings, Laloux's research reveals that people shift from one level of consciousness to the next when they are confronted with a problem that cannot be solved with their current understanding of themselves and the world. The challenge is to be able to move to the next level of complexity in their understanding, which requires a shift in consciousness.

The other option is to cling to the old worldview. This means that when we are faced with the tension and discomfort of the limits of our awareness, we go with the default reaction: we opt for the stability of the known rather than choose the upheaval and discomfort that change requires. But it's important to remember what Kegan and Lahey pointed out: "Just as labor pains are a part of bringing new life into the world, the process of human development, of seeing and overcoming one's previous limitations, can involve pain."[7]

Let's face it—if the evolution of consciousness felt risk-free and pain-free, everyone would already be at the highest levels. It doesn't work that way. The truth about the human experience is that we are constantly faced with a trade-off: *Do we cling to the need for stability and certainty or are we courageous enough to adapt and change?* We know when we are at this juncture when conflict presents itself in our lives, when something isn't working, and when our relationships fall apart. What are we not seeing about how we are contributing to the conflict? Would an expanded consciousness—a broader lens that enables us to see a more complex view of what is happening around us and to us—help us find the highest balcony and reassure us that it's safe to look down?

We need to be willing to trust in the growth process—a process that requires us to believe that our current level of understanding served us well in the past, but its limits are causing trouble for us in the present. Growth requires a leap of faith and a big dose of humility. When faced with the trade-off, what will we do? Will we opt for safety and stability, or will we remind ourselves that we are evolving beings? There is always more to know and learn. Will we be humble enough to understand that what we think we "know" now might soon become only a piece of an expanded understanding of the world that allows us to interact more meaningfully and positively with others and to see ourselves as part of a greater whole?

Laloux reminds us that an organization cannot evolve beyond its leadership's stage of development. What he describes as the most advanced stage of development is consistent with what I have called the *interdependent stage* of dignity consciousness. This stage recognizes that we are evolving beings—that there are always more complex ways of understanding the world. With this broader perspective, we see ourselves as a part of a whole and our lives are viewed as having a purpose that contributes to this greater good.

The connection to a deeper sense of purpose tames the tyranny of the "Me." We realize that the deep wisdom of our "I" prepares us to recognize what that purpose is and to follow its lead, instead of following a path to externally defined success such as the acquisition of wealth, power, or status.

When leaders embody dignity consciousness, the organization stands a good chance of becoming a dignity-conscious organization. Yet a true culture of dignity requires everyone in the organization to become educated about dignity, not just the leadership. What does this look like?

First, everyone in the leadership team must be exposed to basic dignity education that involves an understanding of

• The concept of dignity and how it is different from respect
• Our inherent value and worth, which are internalized in Mandela consciousness

- How to honor dignity (ten essential elements)
- The three Cs (connection to our own dignity, to the dignity of others, and to something greater than ourselves)
- Our hardwired instincts to violate our own dignity (the ten temptations)
- Self-knowledge (the "I" and the "Me")
- Dignity skills (how to give, take, and ask for feedback; how to defend dignity; and how to resolve conflict and heal from wounds to our dignity)

Although this education starts with the leadership team, everyone in the organization needs to be exposed to these concepts. This brings me to another mistake that I made early in my business consulting career—introducing dignity education to the leadership team only.

Without the shared language and understanding of dignity, and a commitment to uphold dignity by the leadership team as well as the employees, it is unlikely that an organizational culture of dignity will take hold and thrive. We will continue to act instinctively in the service of self-preservation when we experience a threat to our dignity, unless we get smart about how to act and react in ways that give us a modicum of control over how we want to be in the world. Do we want to contribute to a culture that understands and nurtures the best of what we are capable of, or do we want to continue being a slave to our hardwired reactions and hope that they may someday produce a different outcome?

For a culture of dignity to succeed, people have to be knowledgeable about what it means to be human and have the courage to act on that knowledge. Elizabeth Samet explains that one of the problems with trust is that it lacks a guarantee.[8] The same is true for dignity. There is no guarantee that embracing dignity consciousness will prevent all conflicts and disruptions in our lives and organizations. What is guaranteed, however, is that without it, we're likely to see more of the same human suffering that only unconditional acceptance of our inherent value and worth can alleviate.

13

Implement a Dignity Education Program for Everyone

When you know better, you do better.
—*Maya Angelou*

In a perfect world, an education program that lays the foundation for establishing a culture of dignity in an organization would include everyone. Because of limited time and resources, however, this is not always possible. One successful program I developed that worked around such limitations was the Dignity Leadership Project at Mount Auburn Hospital in Cambridge, Massachusetts.

My work with the group began when Anne D'Avenas, president of the medical staff, invited me to meet with the hospital's senior management medical staff executive committee, which included chairs of all departments along with the chief executive officer and chief operating officer. The purpose of the meeting was to introduce the project to them and get permission to move forward. They all had read *Dignity* in advance of the meeting and were prepared to discuss how the initiative would be implemented. By the end of the meeting, the executive committee gave me permission to initiate the proposed project, and D'Avenas and I started to think together about who we would include.

We were authorized to include twenty people in the leadership initiative. D'Avenas felt it was important to have representatives from all levels of the organizational hierarchy, so we invited administrators, doctors, nurses, technicians, staff assistants, secretaries, and the head of the environmental services to learn about dignity together. Having people knowledgeable about dignity—I call them "dignity agents"—throughout the organization ensures the ongoing commitment to maintaining a culture of dignity.

Having such a range of participants was a risky move, because the traditional differences in status and power might have created problems for the group. Some of the participants might not have felt safe being with their supervisors or others who had power over them. But this did not happen. There is something extraordinary that takes place when a group learns about dignity together. It creates an intimacy and bond among the participants that I have never seen before in my teaching career. I have taught courses in conflict resolution for twenty-five years, and nowhere else have I experienced the kind of connection that learning about dignity together promotes.

There is something about the topic—maybe it's the recognition of the vulnerability that we all share when it comes to understanding how fragile our sense of worth can be. Maybe it's the awareness of how much suffering is created by injuries to our dignity and how for so long we have not had a language to talk about it. Maybe hearing others speak the truth about what they have been through awakens our willingness to openly and tenderly validate our own unacknowledged pain and suffering.

Whatever the reason, it doesn't take long for everyone to recognize that when it comes to dignity, there is no hierarchy. Regardless of our differences in power and status, we all know the crushing effects of having our dignity violated and the joyful, life-affirming experience of having it honored.

I first discovered this bonding phenomenon when I started presenting the Dignity Model to students. I had no idea that the shared learning experience would foster such deep connections among them. This unintended consequence happened when I first taught my course at the International Center for Cooperation and Conflict Resolution at Teachers College, Columbia University (see Chapter 3).[1] This intensive, three-day class takes place over a weekend. There was a lot of diversity among the participants, many of whom were international students. Very few people knew one another, so when the class began, they were a group of strangers with the common goal of wanting to learn about dignity and how to use it to heal relationships.

I started the class by introducing the basic building blocks of the model. We also did a number of role-play-like reenactments of times when people had experienced a dignity violation. There is nothing like reenacting a real interaction of being treated badly to produce the feeling of having your dignity violated. Maybe it activates our mirror neurons—the part of our brain's architecture that enables us to feel the feelings of others—but everyone watching related to the experiences that were dramatized, and people showed deep empathy and compassion for what participants had been through.[2] Their capacity to connect to each other was immediate and authentic. I was so surprised at not only the healing power of the material but also how quickly people recognized that all of us share the desire for dignity. The experience went beyond finding common ground among them. *It took us to higher ground.*

I then learned that we could think of dignity as our highest common denominator—it is where we can find connection and compassion for one another, no matter our differences. Shared recognition of dignity elevates relationships by giving us a way to find unity beyond our diversity. As important as it is to understand and honor our differences, we need a way to ultimately bring us all back together again. Dignity is that unifying force. It is a shared human yearning with which we can all identify.

I witness and experience for myself the same kind of deep connections with participants whenever I introduce the Dignity Model to groups. Mount Auburn Hospital was no exception. The participants felt safe to talk freely about their dignity experiences in their work environments.

Below is the outline of the dignity education program I developed for the Leadership Training I conducted at the hospital over a six-month period.

Module One: Introduction to the Dignity Model
- Brief history of how the model was developed
- The role of dignity in the exercise of leadership
- Definition of dignity
- Ten elements of dignity

Module Two: Understanding the Evolutionary Roots of Dignity
- Challenges to maintaining dignity
- Ten temptations
- "I" and "Me"

Module Three: Understanding the Impact of Dignity Violations and Honorings

- Early imprints of indignity and their effect on our sense of worth
- Vulnerability/strength inventory (how our early experiences affect our ability to lead with dignity)
- Assessing the dignity concerns in your work groups

Module Four: Leading with Dignity Skills

- Honoring dignity
- Restoring dignity (when you have violated someone)
- Defending dignity (when someone has violated you)
- Giving and receiving feedback
- Self-care

Module Five: Healing and Reconciling Broken Relationships

- Demonstration of a five-step reconciliation process:
- Creating safety
- Telling the story
- Reconnecting to others
- Creating a new story that includes the perspective of the other
- Articulating new learning about oneself and the other

Module Six: Identifying Structural Challenges and Opportunities in Creating a Culture of Dignity

- Identifying systemic issues in the organization that make it difficult to lead with dignity
- What are the dignity trouble spots?
- How to overcome systemic dignity challenges

When we completed these educational sessions, we put together a program in which members of the Dignity Leadership Team would present these lessons to people in their departments. This part of the project was focused on training the team to continue the dignity education after my work was done. D'Avenas remained in the leadership role, organizing members of the team to present what they had learned about dignity to others in the hospital.

I have maintained a relationship with the hospital since leaving the program in D'Avenas's hands. I was asked to present my work at grand rounds, and I have been a speaker at the hospital's leadership academy directed by Patrick Gordon, Becky Logiudice, and Stephanie Page. I was also invited by Andrew Modest, co-chair of the Boston Association of Academic Hospital Medicine, to introduce the Dignity Model to members of the organization. It is safe to say that Mount Auburn Hospital is committed to creating and maintaining a culture of dignity throughout the organization.

In another project with a small nonprofit organization, using the same framework that I have just described, I was able to work with everyone in the organization in a session that included both the leadership team and the employees. Again, dignity leveled the playing field. After several sessions, the employees learned the basics of the model, as well as some dignity skills and tools that I will discuss in Chapter 14.

The most inclusive dignity education project I have been involved with to date is with La Jolla Country Day School, an experience I describe in detail in Chapter 5. There, Gary Krahn has encouraged his faculty to incorporate dignity lessons into their curriculum, and during its orientation week, the school has a program for new faculty that includes an introduction to the Dignity Model—a part of orientation that the new faculty consistently report has the greatest influence on them. Including the students' parents in their efforts has also had a big effect on the success of the dignity education program.

Implementing a dignity education program requires leaders willing to commit time and resources to it. Krahn and his team of educators have done an exemplary job of integrating dignity knowledge and awareness into the school.

Developing dignity consciousness doesn't happen overnight, and it certainly doesn't penetrate an organization without a lot of hard work and dedication to making it a way of life. Changing harmful and dysfunctional patterns of behavior takes time. I have told my clients many times that *dignity work is slow work*. I also point out that they will have good days and bad days—I can personally attest to that. I have been working with the Dignity Model for over a decade, and it still surprises me how I can get caught up in many of the ten temptations, especially taking the bait when someone assaults my dignity. I am very familiar with the rigid righteousness that I can easily slide into when I feel I have been treated unfairly. It lures me right into the justification to lash back and get even. Then again, there are days when I can catch myself, find the balcony, and gain the perspective I need, all because my "I" is present enough to hold back my righteous and outraged "Me."

If everyone in an organization recognizes that we are all works in progress, that developing dignity consciousness takes time, and that we are all up against the same internal struggle to maintain our dignity when our biology wants us to behave differently, we are more likely to feel compassion for others when we see them fall into the evolutionary trap of the ten temptations. If we can look at others and say, "There but for the grace of God go I," we are much more likely to maintain our connection to them instead of crucifying them for something we know could easily happen to us. We are all vulnerable to the same impulses; until we can embrace that truth, we will remain enslaved by them. Accepting our shared human struggle is a choice that requires a knowledge of both our inherent value and our vulnerability—that is, an understanding of our dignity.

14

Assess Dignity Strengths and Weaknesses

An unexamined life is not worth living.
—Plato

Assessing how good an organization's members already are at communicating that they value others, and discovering areas where they need to work on these skills, both interpersonally and at the system level, will help inform and direct the kind of changes required to create a culture of dignity in that organization. At the interpersonal level, the role that self-knowledge plays in the process of creating a healthy, dignity-honoring environment cannot be understated. For all of us, becoming aware of and naming the impact of early violations to our sense of worth and the effects they have on our ability to be in healthy relationships with others can determine how successful we are at leading with dignity. At the systemic level, the dignity framework enables leaders to assess the effect of policy decisions that affect the well-being of all employees.

At the personal level, I ask people to take the vulnerability inventory, which I introduced in Chapter 10. This exercise involves using the ten elements of dignity to determine the extent to which their dignity was honored or violated early in their lives. I ask them to reflect on their *dignity narrative*— how they were treated in significant childhood relationships— with parents, grandparents, siblings, teachers, and classmates.

What does this have to do with leadership? Why is it important to be aware of our early experiences of dignity and indignity? *Because it sets the stage for an understanding of our value and worth.* The purpose is not to blame parents or other significant people in our past, but to uncover the truth about the harm we experienced that prevents us from fully accepting our inherent dignity and, in turn, treating others well. If we fail to reflect on our early experiences, we are likely to unconsciously carry with us a distorted belief in our unworthiness.

As I pointed out earlier, children need ongoing love and attention from caregivers to develop a strong sense of inherent worth.[1] If we don't receive "good enough" care of our dignity early in our lives, self-doubt begins to dominate our inner worlds and can continue to do so well into adulthood.

The awareness of this early impact can help us to identify vulnerabilities in our adult relationships. If we experience the same violations in adulthood that we experienced in childhood, our ability to remain in our "I" frame of mind diminishes and we are likely to lash out at the perpetrator, creating conflict in the relationship. Our "Me" consciousness then takes over and we react, often without thinking, to the memory of the early wound. Reframing the early experiences from an adult perspective—naming the specific violations to our dignity—jumpstarts the healing process by replacing a childlike understanding of our value and worth with a mature, informed, conscious awareness of our inborn dignity.[2] The doors open to Mandela consciousness: the understanding that our dignity is in our hands and no one can take it away from us.

As I have been arguing throughout this book, people who exercise leadership serve themselves and their organizations best when they have a strong sense of their inherent dignity. Those who do not, look for it from external sources in the form of praise and approval of others, and they give up the internal power and stability that comes from knowing their worth. Leaders who are constantly looking for assurance of their dignity from outside sources are distracted from the purpose of leading with dignity—to create an environment where everyone feels seen, valued, and appreciated for who they are and for the contributions they make to the organization. Modeling and upholding the principles of dignity cannot be done when leaders are preoccupied with their own sense of worth.

Another reason that it is important for leaders to have a strong, internalized sense of their dignity is that, without it, it is difficult to take responsibility for one's actions. The temptation to cover up a wrongdoing or mistake is much greater when our sense of worth is on the line. Defending the external threats to dignity becomes a preoccupation and distraction from doing the real work of exercising leadership. As I pointed out earlier, a culture of dignity goes hand in hand with a culture of responsibility and accountability.

The vulnerability inventory takes each of the ten elements of dignity, one by one, and assesses the extent to which these elements were honored or violated during childhood. For example, in introducing the first element, acceptance of identity, I ask, "Do you feel your identity was accepted by the people who mattered to you? Did you feel you were treated differently because of some unchangeable aspect of who you are?" I then ask them to rate, on a scale of one to ten (with ten being the highest), the extent to which they felt this element of dignity was honored in their young lives. Some of the common responses I get to the identity question are:

- I don't feel my father truly accepted who I was. He always talked about wanting a boy and it was clear to me that he was disappointed I am a girl.
- My mother wanted me to be just like her. She had trouble understanding that I had my own desires and hopes for my future that were not the same as what she expected from me.
- My teacher had favorites, and I wasn't one of them. I felt as if he treated me differently because I wasn't as smart as his favorites, and I felt there was nothing I could do to be seen as their equal. I always felt inferior around him.
- My older sister frequently harassed me because she felt that I was always in the spotlight. It wasn't my fault that I was a gifted athlete and I was the star of the soccer team. Instead of supporting me for my talents, she was jealous of them, and when I was young, her hurtful and demeaning behavior toward me left a big scar of self-doubt.
- I can't even describe the countless ways in which I feel people didn't accept my identity because I was of a different race: my classmates, some teachers (not all), and people in general whom I encountered treated me differently. I felt as if I were a second-class citizen all my young life.
- Are you kidding me? Do you really want me to talk about how difficult it was being gay when I was growing up?

Acceptance of identity is such a vulnerable element of dignity. My experience interviewing people with the vulnerability inventory has been quite consistent: *Most people can come up with some significant person or people in their lives who didn't accept them for who they are.* This consistent response illustrates how fragile we all are around the issue of identity and how important it is to consciously think about the effect we have on the people in our lives.

This point was highlighted for me in a conversation I had a few years ago with Jack Nolan, the police commissioner of Dublin, Ireland. I had met with him on a visit to Dublin because he wanted to tell me about a wonderful program that he and his colleagues had developed to protect the migrant workers who came to Ireland to do seasonal agriculture work. He had been told that the migrants were being treated badly, and he wanted to put an end to it. He described his program to me, which, in my terms, was an effort to protect the dignity of the migrants. I congratulated him and told him how impressed I was with what he and his colleagues had done to ensure that the migrants were treated with dignity. He then looked at me and said, "Well, Donna—here is how I see it. I ask myself a question whenever I come in contact with people: *How do I want to make them feel?* I have the power within me to make them feel great and I can also make them feel terrible. It's a matter of conscious choice."[3]

How we treat one another matters—*identity matters*. Experience has led me to believe that many people have an early imprint of indignity when it comes to feeling accepted and good about who they are. Is it any wonder that so few people have a clear and abiding sense of their inherent value and worth—that so few have achieved Mandela consciousness?

Thinking carefully about the effects of early imprints on our dignity and how they have contributed to a disconnection to our inherent value is always a powerful experience. It's not like people change overnight with the realization, but it definitely sets the stage for rethinking self-doubt and reframing our relationship to dignity.

Taking each element separately can help reveal which of them has had the most profound effect on us. When I first took the vulnerability inventory, I saw for the first time how vulnerable I was to the element of *recognition*.

My father was virtually absent in my early life, and even when he was present, he was often emotionally abusive. His addiction to alcohol and gambling was his way of dealing with his own inadequacy and lack of dignity, but it also affected my siblings and me.

When someone in a position of authority is disconnected from his dignity, he is most likely to violate the dignity of those around him. What impact did this have on me? I spent most of my early adult life seeking recognition from male authority figures. I would turn myself inside out to get the recognition that I never got from my father. With the help of the vulnerability inventory and discussions with my friends about it, I could see how much precious time and energy I was wasting on being "seen" by male authority figures. It opened the door to the awareness that as a child, the lack of recognition had had a profound effect on my sense of worth. As an adult reflecting back, I could see what a tragic loss it was and how it had always affected my life. I now know that my dignity is my anchor and no matter how badly someone treats me, it doesn't mean that I am not worthy. *We may betray our dignity, but it will never betray us—it is always there patiently waiting for us to accept it.*

Assessing an organization's dignity strengths and weaknesses follows the same path by using the ten elements of dignity to determine how well the organization honors dignity. I have developed a simple questionnaire that assesses the extent to which employees feel their dignity is honored in the workplace. Taking each element separately, the questionnaire asks, for example, "On a scale of one to ten, how well do you think your identity is accepted in your workplace?" The results of the questionnaire are used as a starting point for follow-up interviews with people.

The assessment helps identify what my friend and organizational consultant Dave Nichol calls "dignity hot spots" in the organization—consistent violations that people report in a particular aspect of the workplace (so in fact, "indignity" hot spots). For example, as I discussed earlier, a dignity hot spot for many of the organizations I have worked with is the element of safety. Very few employees feel safe to speak up when their dignity has been violated for fear of negative backlash from their leaders—a poor performance review or losing their jobs.

Another common dignity hot spot shows up around the issue of fairness and identity. Employees often find reasons to believe that they are not being treated fairly by the company because of some aspect of their identity. A common complaint centers around gender issues. Women often report that they are at a disadvantage when it comes to pay equity.

The leadership team of an organization would be well served to consider the effects of its policy decisions on the dignity of its employees. Again, using the ten elements of dignity as a way to concretely assess the consequences of their decisions, leaders can anticipate the reactions of their employees. For example, does the policy treat everyone fairly? Does it consider the extent to which the policy fosters a feeling of belonging and inclusion? How does the decision affect their *independence*? Will they feel micromanaged, under constant scrutiny at work, or will they experience the freedom and autonomy they need to do their jobs creatively and independently? Does the policy give everyone the benefit of the doubt, or does it assume that people are not trustworthy? To what extent does the policy acknowledge the employees' concerns? These are some of the questions that need to be addressed in order to name and rectify the systemic violations of dignity that can arise in the workplace.

The vulnerability inventory is not only useful for identifying dignity weaknesses; it can also be used to look at the ways in which leaders excel in honoring dignity. For example, asking people to consider the question, "In what ways was your dignity honored as a child?" enables them to see a clear link between being treated well early in their lives and being able to honor the dignity of others.

In one interview, I asked a manager to look at the elements of dignity and tell me which one he felt was most honored in his childhood. He immediately chose the elements of fairness, benefit of the doubt, and understanding. He told me that both of his parents were committed to treating him and his sister fairly when they were children. Even when he or his sister (or both of them) behaved badly, his parents would ask them to explain what happened and sought a deeper understanding of why they did what they did. He told me that he hadn't really thought about this before, but he believed that one of the things he is really good at in his job is treating people fairly and giving them the benefit of the doubt. He said he rarely rushes to judgment when something bad happens with his direct reports. Instead, he digs deeper into what happened and why. This is a perfect example of how our early imprints of dignity can influence our ability to honor the value of others.

Experiences early in life of both dignity and indignity have a profound effect on our sense of worth and on how well-equipped we are to show others that they matter. Most of us have to work hard to implement some elements of dignity leadership (for example, developing an awareness of how our early violations leave us vulnerable to hurting others), while others seem to come naturally. In the end, acknowledging both our strengths and vulnerabilities will give us a more compassionate view of what we are all up against in our common quests to connect with others and to secure and protect our dignity.

15

Address Lingering Wounds
to Dignity

When people have been roughed up, they need acknowledgment
for the suffering they have endured.

—Archbishop Desmond Tutu

Introducing the Dignity Model to an organization is an educational enterprise. I start with the premise that most people have not been exposed to it, which means that learning the building blocks is the first order of business. Once the basics are learned, the next step is to introduce how to apply the language and the lessons to address ongoing, unresolved issues that get in the way of establishing a culture that honors dignity.

As I have pointed out earlier, most of the time I get called into an organization because of workplace conflicts. After I introduce the basics of the Dignity Model, and an assessment is done of the dignity strengths and weaknesses, both among the people and within the organization, addressing the past and lingering wounds to dignity comes next.

The old expression "time heals all wounds" doesn't apply with dignity violations. As Archbishop Tutu told me when we were working together on a project in Northern Ireland, one of the most important things people need when their dignity has been violated is *acknowledgment* for the suffering they have endured. Letting go of past hurts is difficult without it. But what does acknowledgment look like?

Surprisingly, when I ask people to show me what it looks like to acknowledge a dignity violation, few are skilled in doing it. Again, we may be born with dignity, but we're not born knowing how to act like it. *Dignity skills need to be learned.* Next, then, I will show how to acknowledge systemic dignity-related problems—violations of dignity that occur through organizational policies and practices—as well as how to acknowledge interpersonal violations. Both steps are necessary to preserve and protect a culture of dignity in a workplace.

Systemic Acknowledgment

In Chapter 8, I described a problem in which a company was on the verge of bankruptcy, and the senior management asked the employees to take pay cuts to avoid the collapse of the organization. Everyone willingly agreed, and a powerful esprit de corps developed. "Pull together and win together" saw them through the turbulent times.

This spirit changed when the senior management team took big bonuses after the company started doing well and did not restore the pay to the employees. The workers felt betrayed, and the culture had become toxic by the time I was called in to address the conflict. I explained to the management team that they needed to acknowledge the employees' grievances. When they asked me to describe what that would look like, I developed several acknowledgment options for them, ranging from a simple acknowledgment by the management team that the employees were upset, to a full-blown admission of guilt with an apology and a promise to do better.[1]

Here are the options that I gave them:

Option 1: Acknowledgment that their decision to take the bonuses felt like a dignity violation to the employees. We would like to take this opportunity to let you know that we are aware there is a historical grievance regarding the payout of bonuses by the leadership team. We recognize that we asked you to "pull together and win together" when times were hard, so our taking the bonuses later felt unfair, like a betrayal of that agreement. We also recognize that you felt we did not consider what impact our taking the bonuses would have on our agreement and relationship.

Option 2: Acknowledgment with expression of remorse. We would like to take this opportunity to let you know that we are aware there is a historical grievance regarding the payout of bonuses by the leadership team. We recognize that we asked you to "pull together and win together" when times were hard, so our taking the bonuses later felt unfair, like a betrayal of that agreement. We also recognize that you felt we did not consider what impact our taking the bonuses would have on our agreement and relationship. *We feel bad that when we took the bonuses, you felt betrayed and that the actions were unfair, and that you felt we did not consider the impact on you.*

Option 3: Acknowledgment with apology. We would like to take this opportunity to let you know that we are aware there is a historical grievance regarding the payout of bonuses by the leadership team. We recognize that we asked you to "pull together and win together" when times were hard, so our taking the bonuses later felt unfair, like a betrayal of that agreement. We also recognize that you felt we did not consider what impact our taking the bonuses would have on our agreement and relationship. *We would like to apologize for our actions and shortsightedness in not thinking through the consequences of the effects on you.*

Option 4: Acknowledgment with apology and admission of guilt. We would like to take this opportunity to let you know that we are aware there is a historical grievance regarding the payout of bonuses by the leadership team. We recognize that we asked you to "pull together and win together" when times were hard, so our taking the bonuses later felt unfair, like a betrayal of that agreement. We also recognize that you felt we did not consider what impact our taking the bonuses would have on our agreement and relationship. *We realize that we made a mistake and that it damaged our relationship. We would like to apologize for our actions and shortsightedness in not thinking through the consequences of the effects on you, and for any damage to our relationship with you.*

Option 5: Acknowledgment with apology, admission of guilt, and commitment to change the behavior. We would like to take this opportunity to let you know that we are aware that there is a historical grievance regarding the payout of bonuses by the leadership team. We recognize that we asked you to "pull together and win together" when times were hard, so our taking the bonuses later felt unfair, like a betrayal of that agreement. We also recognize that you felt we did not consider what impact our taking the bonuses would have on our agreement and relationship. *We realize that we made a mistake and that it damaged our relationship. We would like to apologize for our actions and shortsightedness in not thinking through the consequences of the effects on you, and for any damage to our relationship with you. We will be taking action to rectify the situation and will take a different approach in the future.*

I presented these options to the management team. Clearly, Option 5 would have been the most satisfying for the employees. Short of that, at the very least starting with the other options could have opened the conversation with the employees. I am sad to note, however, that in this case, none of the options was taken seriously.

Interpersonal Acknowledgment

Another exercise I have developed focuses on how to acknowledge an individual who has experienced a violation to his or her dignity. This exercise does not involve the victim and the perpetrator of the violating interaction, but someone trying to intervene to help the person experiencing the violation. For example, if someone approaches you and is upset because of a hurtful interaction, what do you do?

The goal is to make a connection with the person and to *communicate concern and empathy* for what he or she has endured.

STEP 1: ASK THE PERSON WHAT HAPPENED AND
LISTEN FOR THE DIGNITY VIOLATIONS.

LISTENER: Susan, I can see that you are upset. What happened?

VICTIM: I was in a meeting this morning about a big project that I have been working on for months. My boss introduced a new hire to all of us and told us that he would be heading up the project from now on. My boss was very excited to have such a talented person on board with us, and she was convinced that the outcome of project would be much better now that the new person is directing it. She blindsided me—she didn't tell me in advance that I would no longer be directing the project. She didn't even acknowledge the work that I had done up to that point. If she had told me before the meeting what to expect, I might not have felt so violated, but I felt completely left out of the decision-making, and what is worse, I felt embarrassed in front of my colleagues. The implication was that I wasn't up to the task.

STEP 2: ASK FOR DETAILS WITH
FOLLOW-UP QUESTIONS.

LISTENER: Are you saying that you knew nothing at all about the new hire taking over your job as project manager before the meeting? What was that like for you? (Note that I did not ask her, "How did that make you feel?" Dignity violations are more than a feeling.)

VICTIM: I knew that the new hire was going to be joining the project, but my boss told me nothing about putting him in charge. I'm trying to figure out why my boss would do that to me. She never told me she was unhappy with my work or even suggested that the project wasn't going well. Honestly, I had to hold back tears.

STEP 3: ACKNOWLEDGE THE WRONGDOING.

LISTENER: What happened to you was wrong. I am so sorry you had to go through that.

VICTIM: Thank you for saying that. It really felt wrong.

STEP 4: ASK THE VICTIM HOW SHE WOULD HAVE WANTED TO BE TREATED.

LISTENER: How would you have wanted your boss to handle the situation?

VICTIM: At the very least, I would have wanted her to talk to me about what she was planning to do. In the best case, she would have discussed the project with me and we might have jointly decided that the new hire could bring a fresh perspective to the project. If she had included me in the decision-making, I am quite sure I would not have felt so violated. I would have been part of the problem solving. Instead, I felt embarrassed and I do not feel safe around her anymore.

STEP 5: ASK THE VICTIM WHAT SHE NEEDS AT THAT MOMENT. WHAT DOES SHE WANT TO DO NEXT?

LISTENER: Susan, what do you need at this moment? What would you like to do? (Note that I don't offer to solve the problem for her.)

VICTIM: Thank you so much for being such a good listener. It really helped a lot. I feel validated now. I'd like to talk to my boss when I'm feeling a little less raw. She has told us all that she wants our feedback if we ever feel something isn't right, so I am going to practice my feedback skills and open the conversation with her. Again, thank you for being here with me and giving me support. In the past, I would have just kept this inside. It was really helpful to have you with me to process what happened.

The goal of the listener in this acknowledgment exercise is to help the person who has been violated go through a process that directly addresses and validates the wound she has experienced.

I learned something profound from Paul Farmer, a cofounder of Partners in Health, an international nonprofit organization that provides direct healthcare services for people living in poverty. His approach focuses on the concept of *accompaniment*.[2] The idea is that his job is not to go into a situation as an expert, solving the problem for his patients. Instead, he thinks of himself as an *accompagnateur*—someone who accompanies them through their journey to find health and well-being. It is a way to deliver health care with attention and an awareness of the patients' vulnerability. The accompaniment model is rooted in the notion that we are all equal in dignity, and the most helpful way we can intervene is to join with people to help them recover. There is no asymmetry of power in the healing relationship.

I always think of the role of the listener when someone has her dignity violated as that of an *accompagnateur*. You, the listener, are accompanying the violated person through a healing process, not by telling her what to do, but by being there for her, acknowledging what she already knows. You are there to reassure her that her dignity was violated and to validate her experience. You are not there to fix it with some suggestions for solving the problem. You are there to listen, empathize, and make a healing connection with her.

I have one last point about the acknowledgment exercise. As a listener, *do not tell the victim that you know what she is going through because you had a similar situation and then proceed to tell your story.* We seem to have an instinct to do that—thinking that it would be helpful for the victim to know that we have had a firsthand experience of the same violations. It really doesn't help. The story then becomes about you and not about the victim. You put the victim in a situation in which she needs to switch her attention to you. The acknowledgment exercise is solely about accompanying the victim while she tells her story of what happened. Shifting the focus away from her onto you interrupts the fragile healing process. You want to communicate to her that she is at the center of your concern in the moment. You are there to acknowledge that what happened to her was hurtful and could have been handled differently, in a way that would have preserved dignity.

16

Resolve Current and Future
Conflicts with Dignity

Conflict is the signal that there is something about the relation-ship that needs to change.

One of the most useful tools that I have shared with organizations is how to address conflicts between groups. Conflict is a normal occurrence in the workplace—it is hard to avoid. Having a process to help parties through their difficulties opens up opportunities for growth in the relationship. As the opening quotation suggests, conflict is an indication that there is something in the re-lationship that needs to change. Knowing how to address con-flict with a dignity framework is key to maintaining a healthy culture in which people feel safe to speak up when they run into problems with their colleagues. Knowing how to manage conflicts is a leadership challenge that doesn't come naturally. As with all matters related to dignity, knowing how to address the concerns that so often are at the core of conflicts requires learning.

Defending Dignity

Most of us find it difficult to speak up to others—especially those who have power over us—when they have violated our dignity. We come up with excuses not to speak up, such as "It's not worth the energy," "She doesn't mean that much to me," or "The situation might get worse if I do confront him." Remember that one of the ten temptations is to avoid conflict, for fear of getting hurt again. No wonder it feels so hard to confront others when they have violated our dignity—our biology wants us to protect ourselves at all costs.

But healthy relationships do not handle conflicts by avoiding them. We need to be able to discuss the hurtful behavior with those who have violated our dignity. Here are some helpful steps to implement before speaking up:

- *Acknowledge to yourself that speaking up is difficult* but not impossible, and that it may require practice to get used to the idea.
- *Practice role-playing* with a friend or colleague. When you feel ready, the following are the steps to defending your dignity.

How to Defend Your Dignity
STEP 1: ACKNOWLEDGE TO YOURSELF THAT YOUR DIGNITY HAS TAKEN A HIT

- Recognize that your "Me" has been injured and that it wants to lash back and get even, or to withdraw from the relationship.

- Remember the ninety-second rule, and give the stress hormones that are coursing through your body a chance to clear out. Push the pause button and let your anger run its course.
- Get to the metaphorical balcony—recognize that your "I" needs to take charge so that you don't respond by taking the bait and returning the violation.

STEP 2: SWITCH THE DEFAULT REACTION FROM REVENGE TO SELF-REFLECTION

- Ask yourself: "Is there anything I might have done to contribute to this failed interaction? Is there any possibility that I might have unknowingly violated his or her dignity?" (Note that even if you did do something to the other person, you still may have suffered a dignity violation.)

STEP 3: RESPOND TO THE VIOLATOR

- If you think you might have contributed to the conflict, take responsibility: "I realize that I might have offended you when I said _____. I am sorry for that." (Do not say "but" and then proceed to describing your own violation. Saying "but" deletes all the benefit of the apology taken on your part.) Pause and let the person respond.
- Next, address the hurt you experienced: "Maybe you are not aware of it, but what you said in the meeting about me was hurtful (explain the incident). My relationship with you is important to me, and I'm concerned that if I let the hurtful remarks pass without talking to you about how I feel, it might jeopardize our relationship. I want to give you the benefit of the doubt that you weren't aware of the impact of your comments."

My experience is that when you approach a violator in this way, saying that the relationship is important to you, and that you want to give the offender the benefit of the doubt that she was unaware of how hurtful the violation was, she will feel disarmed and at least somewhat open to this feedback. She was almost certainly not expecting to hear that you care about your relationship or that you want to give her the benefit of the doubt—instead she's probably been bracing herself for an unpleasant encounter in which you return the harm. Nor is she prepared for your taking responsibility for possibly violating her dignity. Your deeply humanizing response, which I call a "surprise attack," is just what is needed when dignity violations put us on a fast track to disconnecting not only from the suffering relationship, but also from the offender's human vulnerability.

It goes without saying that it is nearly impossible to do this when your "Me" is in charge of your behavior and the stress hormone is still preparing you for a fight or a flight. A few trips up to the balcony help a lot, along with practicing the encounter with a friend or colleague.

Addressing Intergroup Conflict: Dignity Dialogues

A manager asked me to help him with an ongoing conflict that he was trying to resolve between two factions in his team. One group worked on the technical (IT) aspects of his department, and the other group handled the interface with customers. The manager told me that he had found it challenging to build a bridge between the two groups because they had such diverse talents and there was little overlap between them. He had heard about the dignity work I was doing in other departments and asked whether I would work with him to try to address the issues that divided the team. He thought that underlying dignity violations were fueling the conflict.

I have developed what I call dignity dialogues to help groups find a way out of their conflicts. My methodology was inspired by the work of my mentor at Harvard, Herbert Kelman.[1] As a social psychologist specializing in the social psychological dimensions of international conflict, he developed the Interactive Problem-Solving Approach that he used to bring Israelis and Palestinians together for dialogue. The approach focuses on the underlying, unmet psychological human needs that contribute to conflict. My adaptation of the method focuses on the unaddressed dignity violations that fuel the inability of parties to end their conflicts.

Dignity dialogues are an educational approach to addressing conflict. When I work with groups who are unable to get along, I quickly discover that they typically know next to nothing about dignity, except that they all agree that it is important to them.

The first step of a dignity dialogue, then, is to learn the basic building blocks of the Dignity Model, which I have described in detail earlier in the book. These building blocks include the definition of dignity, Mandela consciousness, the ten elements of dignity, the three Cs, the ten temptations to violate dignity, and self-knowledge of the "I" and the "Me." What is most powerful about this first step is that groups of participants *learn about dignity together.* I tell them that during the first step of the process, they will all be sharing the identity "students of dignity." I ask them to briefly suspend other aspects of their identity (such as members of the IT team or the customer service team) until they have learned together the basics of the Dignity Model.

This step also includes experiential exercises that involve

reenactments of dignity violations, which I have described earlier in the book (see Chapter 13). I ask for volunteers to describe a time, early in their lives, when their dignity was violated. I ask about their childhood experiences because they are powerful and tend to create a lasting effect on one's sense of worth. These exercises that focus on childhood violations also take participants out of the present, which is filled with current violations that are harder to empathize with when both sides feel like adversaries.

One of the goals of the reenactments is to try to restore the natural capacity for empathy that we typically feel for one another.[2] One of the first things to go with groups in conflict is empathy. The disconnection brings out what my colleague at Harvard Law School, Dan Shapiro, calls the "tribes effect" that creates an "us versus them," adversarial mentality.[3]

Observing others reenact painful injuries to their dignity can ignite our mirror neurons and make us feel the heartbreaking effects of their violations.[4] It can also restore the empathy that was lost in the conflict, turning adversaries back into fellow human beings.

Seeing the suffering of others can trigger something deep in us. Yes, we might feel their pain, but does observing the suffering cause us also to reach further into our shared human experience? Do we experience a moment of recognition of a tragic aspect of what it means to be human—that we have yet to wake up to the reality that we are all so fragile, yet we are treating one another as if we weren't? Most of the time we can live our lives in denial of all the indignities that are happening around us. But when we are face to face with someone's real-life experience of being treated badly, it is hard to look away.

One of the most compelling examples of the power of face-to-face interactions is a video entitled *Look Beyond Bor-*

ders, made by Amnesty International.[5] It demonstrates how just four uninterrupted minutes of eye contact between people can create a deep human connection. I urge you to take a look at this powerful demonstration of what we humans are capable of, if we take the time to look at and listen to what is happening inside the lived experience of others.

The combination of the shared learning and the recognition of the shared pain and suffering brought on by hurtful violations to dignity sets the stage for the dialogue to begin. It goes without saying that the facilitator of these dialogues needs to be trained in basic facilitation skills. Here is a typical agenda for a dignity dialogue after the participants learn the building blocks of the model.

SESSION 1: INTRODUCING THE DIGNITY DIALOGUE

In this session, I explain to the participants that the purpose of the dialogue is to strengthen the relationship between the two groups. I remind them that we will be using a dignity framework to guide our work together, drawing on the learning that we gained as "students of dignity."

Establish the ground rules for discussion. The first ground rule is *confidentiality.* No attributions of who said what are to be made outside of the sessions, unless everyone agrees that doing so is okay. Second, I tell them to *listen to understand and speak to be understood.* I ask them to ask themselves: *Are you listening or waiting to speak?* I then always ask the participants if there are other ground rules they would like to add.

Defining the shared dignity purpose. After the ground rules are agreed on, we begin our first working session. The goal is to *define the "dignity purpose" of the participants' work to-*

gether as a team. The discussion uses the ten elements of dignity to guide their framing of the purpose. We start by defining the general purpose of the team (for example, to provide a technically efficient way for customers to gain access to the company's services). The next step is to articulate how promoting dignity could contribute to a successful outcome of their teamwork.

SESSION 2: IDENTIFYING DIGNITY ISSUES, BY GROUP

The goal of this session is to clarify and identify the problems in the relationship between the two groups. One of the most common mistakes people make when trying to resolve conflict is to rush to find a solution to the problem before having a clear sense of what caused the breakdown in the relationship. The felt need to "fix" what is wrong is compelling, but without an accurate assessment of what is creating and fueling the problem, the solution will not lead to an enduring end to the conflict. With a dignity-based approach, the next step is instead to identify and discuss the violations that both sides have experienced.

At the beginning of the session, the members of one of the groups are asked to talk about the dignity violations they have experienced in their interactions at work. Each person has an opportunity to tell his or her story. I ask them not to name names but still to describe in detail the kinds of violations they have experienced. The other group is instructed to sit quietly and listen to the stories, asking questions only for clarification. It is a time not to debate the issues, but to listen and gain a deeper understanding of what the other side has experienced.

When Group 1 feels that they have finished telling their stories, someone from Group 2 is asked to go to the board and write down what the group heard from Group 1—the dignity violations they felt they had experienced in the relationship. While members of Group 2 are writing down what they heard, the members of Group 1 are not allowed to speak or otherwise correct them. When they have finished writing the list of what they heard, Group 1's members are given the opportunity to amend the list.

Next it is Group 2's turn to tell their stories about ways in which they felt their dignity has been violated in the relationship. All the steps (telling their stories, repeating back by the other side, and editing the list) are repeated for Group 2.

SESSION 3: RESPONDING TO STORIES

Up to this point, the facilitator has not allowed the groups to discuss or respond to the issues that were raised during the previous session. This session is an opportunity for them to react to what they heard and to gain a deeper understanding of the issues, but *it is not the time to come up with solutions*. The goal of this session is to open the space for *acknowledgment and/or apology* by both parties of the dignity violations they heard the other side describe. It is an opportunity for them to switch their default setting from blaming the other side for a wrongdoing to taking responsibility for the harm they themselves have done.

SESSION 4: FINDING SOLUTIONS AND NEW STEPS

This session begins with the question "What can our side do to avoid violating the dignity of the other side and to improve the working relationship?" The goal of this session is to find solutions to the issues that were raised. Now that the groups have a deeper understanding of the violations they have both endured, steps that they take to repair the relationship will be framed in terms of protecting and promoting a culture of dignity. For example, if one of the concerns had to do with a failure to include each other in important decisions that affect the whole team and its purpose, they would commit to erring on the side of inclusion in the future. The groups establish new "rules of engagement" that are based on the ten elements of dignity.

SESSION 5: REFLECTING ON THE ORIGINAL DIGNITY
PURPOSE AND THE DIGNITY DIALOGUE EXPERIENCE

In the final session, both groups are asked to look again at the dignity purpose they developed in the beginning of the workshop to see whether there is anything they'd like to change. Then the groups are asked to reflect on what they learned about themselves and the other group after going through the dignity dialogue. The last question I ask them to answer is "What happened in the workshop that had the greatest effect on you?" Each person answers the question while the others listen. They are also invited to say anything else about what it was like for them in the workshop.

If the organization hasn't already conducted a system-wide dignity education program, these dialogue workshops typically take two days—one for the initial dignity education component and one for the dialogue itself.

I am reminded of a quotation from Winston Churchill: "Criticism may not be agreeable, but it is necessary. It fulfills the same function as pain in the human body. It calls attention to an unhealthy state of things." Establishing a process and a methodology to address conflicts and allow for constructive criticism in the workplace is one of the essential elements of a healthy, dignity-honoring culture.

When an organization commits to institutionalizing a way to address conflicts as they arise, the process is normalized. In contrast, if conflict is avoided and allowed to fester, it creates a toxic work environment where people do not feel safe to speak and they do not feel that their concerns have been recognized and addressed. Without a way to be listened to and heard, people who have been violated often resort to gossiping about the perpetrators, polluting the workplace environment with negativity. Matthew Feinberg, Joey Cheng, and Robb Willer sum it up beautifully, "Gossip represents a widespread, efficient and low-cost form of punishment."[6] Robert Sapolsky, author of *Behave: The Biology of Humans at Our Best and Worst* says: "Gossip (with the goal of shaming) is a weapon of the weak against the powerful."[7] And as Daniel Kahneman asks, "Why should we be concerned with gossip? Because it is much easier, as well as far more enjoyable, to identify and label the mistakes of others than to recognize our own."[8] If a mechanism is in place whereby people feel their concerns can be acknowledged and addressed, the temptation to talk disparagingly about those who have committed dignity violations could be eliminated.

Normalizing ways to address conflict is at the core of maintaining a safe culture for everyone to speak up, be recognized, and take responsibility for hurtful behavior. Most important, it gives people an opportunity to learn something about themselves that only others can see. Because we all have blind spots, we need the perspective of others in order to continue to develop into more dignity-conscious human beings.

Without conflict and a healthy way to address it, we remain in an arrested state of development. If we want to grow and flourish, we should welcome having a mirror held up to us in a way that can expand our ability to preserve our dignity and the dignity of those around us.

17

The Dignity Pledge

The purpose of every great business is usually something deeper and more transcendent, aligned with having a positive impact on the world and on the lives of people.

—Bob Chapman and Raj Sisodia

Most of the organizations with which I have worked have embraced the idea that dignity plays an important role in the well-being and health of the workplace culture. I make it clear that dignity has a significant effect on people as well as on the organization's capacity to create meaning and purpose for those who are part of it. I remind them that dignity is about three things: *connection, connection, and connection* (the three Cs): connection to our own dignity, to the dignity of others, and to the dignity of something greater than ourselves. If an organization commits to establishing a culture of dignity within the system, these dimensions of dignity are seamlessly woven together.

To formalize the commitment to dignity, I ask organizations to come up with a written document that describes their pledge to create a work environment that honors the three dimensions of dignity.

A few years ago, I wrote a simple dignity pledge for an organization that was struggling with relationship problems. From that point on, I have used it to show clients what their pledge to honor dignity might look like. Organizations use it as a starting point for the development of their own written commitment.

Dignity Pledge

We, the people of (_____), aspire to create a culture of dignity in our organization by embodying the following principles:

Dignity Matters

We are a dignity-conscious company that recognizes the importance of treating ourselves, each other, and the customers we serve in a way that honors their value and worth and the significant role they play in the organization.

Identity Matters

We want our employees and customers to be proud to be a part of an organization that puts recognition of their value and worth at the center of our brand and image.

Leadership Matters

We are a company whose leaders aspire to lead with dignity and promote an organizational culture of learning through self-reflection and accountability.

People Matter

We are a company whose employees aspire to treat each other with dignity and promote an organizational culture of learning through self-reflection and accountability.

Relationships Matter

We are a company that wants strong connections with all our work groups, and we are committed to building those relationships on a foundation of dignity.

Workplace Matters

We are a company that people want to work for and where they enjoy their jobs and each other. We strive to make the work environment one where people feel free to "speak up" and be heard without fear of recrimination.

Conflict Matters

We are a company that recognizes that conflict is a normal occurrence and is a useful signal of the need for change. We are committed to establishing dialogue processes so that conflicts can be managed in a dignified way, ensuring that people's concerns are heard and acknowledged. We recognize that managing conflict and the need for change is key to the company's continued growth and prosperity.

The Kellogg Institute for International Studies at Notre Dame University has developed an exceptional example of a dignity pledge. Under the leadership of Paolo Carozza, the director of the institute, and Steve Reifenberg, executive director, we implemented a dignity project for all the staff. After working with them on the dignity education component of the project, they were given the task of creating a written declaration of their commitment to creating a dignity-honoring culture. Here is what they came up with:

Human Dignity in Our Work:
Principles Adopted by the Staff of the Kellogg
Institute for International Studies

The Kellogg Institute is a place where we seek to honor human dignity in all that we do. Recognizing that the dignity of each one of us is interdependent with the dignity of others with whom we work and whom we serve, we are committed to advancing the human dignity of every person in every aspect of the Institute's mission of research, teaching and learning, and service to the University of Notre Dame and to the world.

Therefore, we have adopted the following principles by which we seek to guide our work, both individually and as a community:

1. We are committed to recognizing that our own human dignity requires each of us to take our personal work seriously by seeking meaning and aspiring to excellence in all that we do, by continuing to learn and develop professionally, and by aiming to make a positive contribution to the mission of the Institute as a whole in all of our work.

2. We are committed to honoring the dignity of all our colleagues and of all those with whom the Institute interacts (students, visitors, etc.) by regarding one another always as persons of equal and inherent value, and by treating one another with fairness, honesty, openness, and trust.

3. We are committed to building and maintaining a community that fosters mutual respect among all

of us, that values the unique contributions and
responsibilities of every member of our community, and that aims to enhance and develop the
creativity, empowerment, independence, and development of each person in the context of his or
her work responsibilities.

4. We are committed to making our environment
one in which communication among us is free
and open, where each person feels safe in raising
and discussing any issue of common concern or
interest, and where we listen sincerely, carefully,
and charitably to one another.

5. We are committed to holding ourselves and one
another accountable for these principles, and
to helping one another grow in our capacity to
honor the dignity of every person consistently
and fully.

The Kellogg Institute's set of dignity principles reflects
their purpose and the interdependence of dignity. All three
connections were included: its pledge honors their individual dignity, the dignity of others, and something greater than
themselves ("we are committed to advancing the human dignity of every person in every aspect of the Institute's mission of
research, teaching and learning, and service to the University
of Notre Dame and to the world"). To this day, the Kellogg
Institute is consciously working to maintain its commitment
and aspiration to defend and protect dignity in all its manifestations.

Given all that we are up against as humans (including
our instincts to act in the service of self-preservation over connection to others when we perceive a threat to our well-being),

choosing to commit to our highest common denominator (our shared yearning to be treated with dignity) demands our personal best. The internal challenges we face are formidable. As E. O. Wilson pointed out, our inherited mental architecture sets us up for living a life of ruthless ambivalence.[1] Do we let our hardwired instincts for self-preservation (our tyrannical "Me") take over, or do we struggle to keep our "I" in the driver's seat so that we can remain on higher ground and let the better angels of our nature be in charge of our decision-making? Doing what is right is a conscious choice, especially when our instinct is to think that we know better.

In *The Power of Ideals: The Real Story of Moral Choice,* William Damon and Anne Colby make the case that people's commitment to ideals such as truthfulness, humility, and faithfulness play a significant role in moral decision-making.[2] This point may seem obvious, but these authors are responding to a growing body of research showing that our moral judgments are driven by biologically driven instincts that determine how we act.[3] In the authors' words: "One of the salient features of the new science view is its claim that moral choices are generally irrational, rarely (if ever) guided by moral understanding."[4]

Damon and Colby are not arguing against the role of biological forces in moral thinking. Their point is that they are not the only contributor. Their book showcases several people who have behaved in exemplary ways, in spite of the internal biological forces that are at play when we are confronted with a difficult moral judgment. Yes, it is hard to overcome the pull of our evolutionary inheritance, but it can be done.

Damon and Colby argue vigorously that education and a commitment to ideals play a big role in guiding our behavior. They point out that "much of everyday behavior is automatic and reflexive. But even the most routine, seemingly automatic habits and intuitions owe a debt to conscious learning."[5] They tell us that education can help us manage the biological forces that are part of the human moral experience, guiding us with the ideals and virtues that can help us make choices that empower us to do what is right. Their three ideals—truthfulness, humility, and faithfulness—are consistent with living a dignified life. I would add that a commitment to honoring dignity is a universal ideal to which anyone can aspire. In my travels worldwide, I have yet to meet a person who doesn't care about dignity or think it is important in our lives.

Educating ourselves about matters of dignity is the first step toward gaining a deeper understanding of ourselves and the forces we are battling when trying to maintain our commitment to it. The ten temptations to violate our own and others' dignity are such forces. It may not be our fault that we have this evolutionary legacy, but it is our responsibility to know these temptations, understand them, and use our more evolved consciousness to control them. *The better part of dignity is restraint.*

Organizations have the power to help their members develop a higher consciousness of dignity. Making a pledge and commitment to establish a culture in which employees consciously try to uphold their duty to dignity helps them in their own growth process. We spend so much time in the workplace, why not leverage it to struggle together to overcome dignity's many challenges?

In *Everybody Matters,* Bob Chapman and Raj Sisodia chronicle Bob's pledge as the chief executive officer of his company, Barry-Wehmiller, to do what he could in his organization to positively influence the lives of his employees. As they write, "The purpose of every great business is usually something deeper and more transcendent, aligned with having a positive impact on the world and on the lives of people."[6] Although the authors never mention the word *dignity,* I kept thinking while I read the book that Barry-Wehmiller was a dignity-honoring environment, and that Chapman leads with dignity. Caring for and recognizing the inherent value and worth of his people was always on his mind. He made conscious choices on a daily basis to stay true to his (dignity-honoring) values.

In organizations where the leadership is less thoughtful, too, a dignity pledge clearly defines the *rules of engagement,* serving as a written and agreed-on document that provides a check and balance for all, but especially those who have the power to potentially abuse their authority. The pledge holds everyone accountable.

As Damon and Colby remind us, there are many examples of people who have lived out their commitment to something greater than themselves, whether it was to social justice and equality, truth, humility, or faith in a transcendent power. They all were driven by something deeper than their own self-interest. They had their three connections to dignity aligned. They knew their worth, but they also knew that their worth was directly connected to the dignity of others and to the dignity of the greater good. Is a commitment to the ideal of upholding dignity something everyone can aspire to? As Damon and Colby suggest, with thoughtful education, most of us can learn to choose to do what is right.

18

Normalize Dignity Learning and Practice

We can do better.

When I introduce the dignity education component to organizations, I always get the same reaction: You have put words to our problem. It all sounds like common sense, so why has it taken so long for someone to shine a light on it?

All I know is that dignity has been following me around all my life. When I was a child, I could feel the gravitational force of indignity. Not only did it pull me down, but I could feel it all around me. I didn't have enough cognitive sophistication then to put words to it, but I knew—with childlike intuitive clarity—that there had to be a better way. It wasn't until I saw and experienced the devastating effects of indignity on a grand scale, however—when people were willing to go to war and endure years of conflict and suffering to regain it—that it finally woke me up to doing something about it. Now, after more than a decade working with people and organizations, I can say with confidence: We can do better.

We have what it takes to learn how to avoid the hurtful, often unconscious ways of responding to threats to our well-being. We can learn how to restrain ourselves from the impulse for self-preservation and choose to preserve our dignity and the dignity of others instead. Yes, we can do better, but we have to give dignity education our full attention. It is possible to learn how to manage all the issues that get us into trouble in our relationships and how to make conscious choices about the way we want to be with others in the world. It is our responsibility to increase the expectations of what we are capable of, rather than hope that others will change.

We don't naturally know how to read, write, or do myriad other intellectual feats, not to mention play music, ride bicycles, or become outstanding athletes. Think of all the time and attention we put into learning, even exceling at, these skills. If we put the same kind of effort into learning about ourselves and what it takes to embrace our dignity and to become good at being in relationships with others, we might see a world with more love, more joy, and certainly less conflict. Dignity-conscious organizations would be experienced not only as places to earn an income, but also as cultures that offer opportunities for self-expansion and development. They would also offer a testing ground for learning how to connect with others in a way that honors and protects dignity—our own as well as that of others and the organization.

What are the skills that need both to be learned and to become a normal part of the way people interact with one another? Individuals, as well as organizational cultures, that promote and defend dignity are able to

1. **Honor one's own and others' dignity.** Using the ten elements of dignity as a guide, dignity-conscious cultures make clear what the rules of engagement are in the organization (see Chapter 1).

2. **Defend one's dignity with skill and humanity when necessary.** In dignity-conscious cultures, participants recognize the importance of not taking the bait; they avoid returning the harm done when a dignity violation occurs (see Chapter 16).

3. **Give, receive, and ask for feedback.** Members of cultures that are mindful of dignity recognize that we all have blind spots and that everyone needs the eyes of others to see what we cannot see on our own (see Chapter 7).

4. **Resolve conflict with dignity.** Dignity-conscious cultures identify conflict as a signal for the need to change something in the relationship (see Chapter 16).

5. **Take responsibility for violating the dignity of others**. It is essential to understand that saving face is too costly: dignity-conscious cultures realize that it risks a loss of valuable trust in relationships (see Chapter 11).

In addition to acquiring these skills, a successful dignity-conscious organizational culture demonstrates the willingness to put the knowledge into practice. The challenges to this kind of leadership are significant. External forces work against institutionalizing and normalizing dignity practice, with the most significant of these being lack of exposure to dignity education. Also, as organizational consultant Dick Cocozza points out, the stated focus of many organizations is accomplishing their strategic goals, and if honoring dignity is not woven into these goals, the dignity of employees may be seen as distracting from the organization's interests.[1] As if that is not enough, the internal forces that I have described throughout this book are equally formidable.

Making the crossing to dignity consciousness can be treacherous, because we are fighting powerful cultural and evolutionary forces, but after reaching the other side, the rewards far outweigh the risks. Safety and freedom await in a place where people are willing to speak up, to be their authentic selves, and to explore the boundaries of what they know, all in the service of continued growth and development instead of a relentless impulse for self-preservation. We can do better if we normalize what everyone wants—to live together in a world where we all matter, and where our worth is recognized and appreciated wherever we are.

19

Humanity Ascending

The Rewards of Leading with Dignity

Someday, after mastering the winds, the tides, and gravity, we shall harness the energies of love and then, for a second time in the history of the world, we will have discovered fire.
—*Pierre Teilhard de Chardin*

In 2016, I was asked to give a dignity workshop at the Harvard Divinity School to a group of graduate students from all over the university who were enrolled in a course entitled "Transformative Leadership and Spiritual Development: Cultivating Our Capacities as Practitioners of Sustainable Peace." As part of the course, Elizabeth Lee Hood, a workshop organizer, asked me to share with the group my own spiritual development and how it has affected my conflict-resolution practice.

I explained that I had recently had a profound personal insight: after twenty-five years of working in the field of international conflict, it wasn't conflict I was interested in. What I really cared about was love. It had taken me a while to figure out that at its core, conflict is created in the absence of love, and if we want to bring an end to violence and suffering in the world, we need to get better at loving.

At the heart of dignity is love. Over the past decade, I have refocused and reframed my conflict work and begun a new chapter of my life and career. I have created the Dignity Model, committing myself to learning, understanding, educating, and practicing the act of loving through the honoring of dignity.

As simple and straightforward as that sounds, my path took many twists and turns, but in the end, what I know now is that love is so much more than a feeling. Insights from Barbara Fredrickson's remarkable book *Love 2.0: Creating Happiness and Health in Moments of Connection* gave me the evidence I needed to make the connection between love and dignity.[1] She describes the body's reaction to experiencing what she calls positivity resonance, in which two people connect in a genuine way. She states that love is connection. The pleasant and often fleeting moments when two people have a positive experience together is what she calls love. After years researching the science of love, she has concluded that genuine connection with others creates trust, loyalty, and the desire to spend time with them, not to mention all the beneficial health effects.

If love is connection, then the experience of having our dignity honored is what creates the connection. It reminds me of the powerful statement by Jack Nolan, the police commissioner of Dublin about whom I wrote in Chapter 14. He certainly didn't know the science behind his words, but when he asked, "How do I want to make people feel?" he was expressing his deep wisdom that connects the ideas of treating people with dignity and making people feel cared for and loved. Fred-erickson makes it very clear that you can express an act of love to anyone, even a stranger. Honoring their dignity is a fast and easy way to do it.

My answer to the class about my spiritual development was that I strongly believe honoring dignity is a spiritual prac-tice, because in my mind, spirituality is about connection. As Gregory Fricchione points out, "Spirituality is in large meas-ure summarily described by its embodiment in one word, *love,* which is experienced as the feeling force of connection. Being spiritual implies a loving connection to our fellow human be-ings, to our world, to someone or something larger than our-selves."[2]

The act of honoring the three dignity connections—to our own dignity, to the dignity of others, and to the dignity of something greater than ourselves—is at the heart of living a spiritual life. Dignity practice is humbling, yet expansive; joyful, yet reflective; outward reaching, yet inwardly reward-ing. Everything expands when these three connections are in alignment.

My friend and colleague Evelin Lindner believes that we must redefine what is love. She, too, feels that it is more than a feeling—it is a principle around which we should live and organize our lives and the world.[3] She feels that love—forceful, fierce, and big—is the only true antidote to humiliation in all of its manifestations. Love is what heals. It is also a skill, a set of rules, an institutional frame for organizations and wherever people cluster. Love has force, she tells us. It is a force that can be used or wasted. The time has come to mobilize the forces of love and dignity and bring an end to preventable human suffering.

But these forces cannot be mobilized without education

and without leaders who are willing and able to create the kind of environments necessary for love and dignity to flourish. Maia Szalavitz and Bruce Perry remind us that the gifts of our biology are a potential, not a guarantee.[4] Even though we are wired for love and connection, we still have to put in time and effort to learn how to make them second nature and a way of life.

This book is an attempt to bring into focus the power and potential of organizations to create work environments that contribute to human flourishing and human development. Martin Seligman and the positive psychology movement have made significant contributions to our understanding of the components of happiness, well-being, and human growth, but surprisingly, the concept of dignity is not mentioned in his writings.[5] His five elements of well-being are positive emotion, engagement, meaning, positive relationships, and accomplishment. Yet what about being grounded in your sense of worth? What about knowing that your dignity is in your own hands and no one can take it away from you? What about the role dignity plays in creating positive relationships? It seems that it would be difficult to truly experience a profound sense of well-being without being firmly grounded in an abiding self-acceptance. Dignity-conscious organizations, as I have described them in this book, give rise to all of Seligman's five elements. They provide the emotional infrastructure within people and within organizations that is necessary to promote human flourishing.[6]

Imagine what progress we could make at improving our ability to sustain loving relationships if more leaders of organizations made the commitment to lead with dignity and pledged to create a culture that sustained and nurtured everyone's value and worth. Organizations and workplaces could be the

platform where dignified human connections are cultivated—
places where the likelihood of triggering our self-preservation
instincts is reduced and, instead, our inborn desire to be in
loving relationships with others is nurtured.

My hope with this book is that more leaders of organizations will be exposed to dignity education and will feel inspired
to find their own alignment of the three Cs. Institutionalizing a
commitment to dignity starts with making a conscious choice
that dignity matters, educating everyone about it, and pledg-
ing to do what it takes to develop, sustain, and nurture this
higher ground. If we have a part to play in humanity's ascent to
this higher ground, we'll need people at the forefront who are
prepared to lead with and for dignity.[7] I know of a battalion of
third-graders at Trinity Valley School who are already taking
up this challenge. How about you?

Notes

Introduction

1. Panksepp and Biven, *Archaeology of Mind.*
2. Heifetz, *Leadership without Easy Answers.*
3. I worked with Archbishop Desmond Tutu co-facilitating a BBC television series *Facing the Truth,* where we brought together victims and perpetrators of the conflict in Northern Ireland to help promote reconciliation between the Catholic and Protestant communities. It was a three-part series that aired on BBC UK and BBC World in March 2006.
4. Samet, *Leadership.*
5. Fuller, *Somebodies and Nobodies.*
6. Edmondson, *Teaming.*
7. Hicks and Waddock, "Dignity, Wisdom, and Tomorrow's Ethical Business Leaders."

1
How to Honor Dignity

1. See https://www.humiliationstudies.org for more information on the Human Dignity and Humiliation Studies network.
2. Lindner, "Concept of Human Dignity"; Lindner, *Emotion and Conflict;* Lindner, *Gender, Humiliation, and Global Security;* Lindner, *Making Enemies.*
3. Lieberman, *Social.*
4. Harari, *Sapiens.*
5. Hartling and Lindner, "Healing Humiliation."

6. Eisenberger, Lieberman, and Williams, "Does Rejection Hurt?"

7. Bazerman, *Power of Noticing.*

8. Szalavitz and Perry, *Born for Love.*

9. Pirson, *Humanistic Management.*

10. Von Kimakowitz et al., "Introducing This Book and Humanistic Management."

11. Giles, "Most Important Leadership Competencies."

12. Valcour, "Power of Dignity in the Workplace."

13. Hodson, *Dignity at Work.*

14. Porath, *Mastering Civility.*

2
How to Avoid Violating Dignity

1. Mlodinow, *Subliminal.*

2. Buss, *Evolutionary Psychology.*

3. Wilson, *Social Conquest of the Earth.*

4. Barkow, *Missing the Revolution.*

5. Dunbar and Barrett, *Handbook of Evolutionary Psychology.*

6. Haidt, *Righteous Mind.*

7. Hartling and Lindner, "Healing Humiliation."

8. Quotation by Edward O. Wilson in Wilson, *Meaning of Human Existence,* 179.

9. Quotation by Edward O. Wilson in Wilson, *Social Conquest of the Earth,* 248.

10. James, *Principles of Psychology.*

3
Dignity's Depth and Breadth

1. For more information about the International Center for Cooperation and Conflict Resolution (ICCCR), see http://icccr.tc.columbia.edu.

4
Leadership and Human Development

1. Samet, *Leadership.*

2. Pfeffer, *Leadership BS.*

3. Heifetz and Linsky, *Leadership on the Line.*
4. Kegan and Lahey, *Immunity to Change.*
5. Ibid.
6. Davidson with Begley, *Emotional Life of Your Brain.*
7. Kegan and Lahey, *An Everyone Culture,* 9.
8. Hartling and Lindner, "Healing Humiliation."
9. Hicks, *Dignity.*

5
How to Educate Future Leaders about Dignity

1. For more information about Trinity Valley School, see: https: //www
.trinityvalleyschool.org. Insights from Gary Krahn are from personal communications with the author.

2. Information about Carol Gramentine's approach and her reflections
about students are from her personal communications with the author.

3. For more information about La Jolla Country Day School, see: https: //
www.ljcds.org.

4. The quotations by teachers in the next paragraphs are from personal
communications with the author.

5. For more information about Berkeley Carroll School, see: https: //www
.berkeleycarroll.org.

6. Mike Wilper's teachings about dignity and quotations from students
are from his personal communications with the author.

6
Demonstrate and Encourage Lifelong Learning
and Development

1. Robinson and Aronica, *Creative Schools.*
2. Thoreau, *Civil Disobedience and Other Essays.*
3. Dweck, *Mindset.*
4. David, *Emotional Agility.*
5. Kegan and Lahey, *An Everyone Culture.*

7
Set the Tone

1. Miller, *Toward a New Psychology of Women.*
2. Mlodinow, *Subliminal.*
3. Edmondson, "Psychological Safety and Learning Behavior in Work Teams."
4. Edmondson, *Teaming.*
5. Stone and Heen, *Thanks for the Feedback.*
6. Tannenbaum, "But I Didn't Mean It."
7. Brown, *Daring Greatly.*

8
Cultivate Trust

1. Bal and de Jong, "From Human Resource Management to Human Dignity Development."
2. De Nalda, Guillen, and Pechuan, "Influence of Ability, Benevolence, and Integrity."
3. Covey and Conant, "Connection between Employee Trust and Financial Performance."
4. Guillén and González, "Ethical Dimension of Managerial Leadership."
5. Sapolsky, *Behave.*
6. Szalavitz and Perry, *Born for Love.*
7. Zak, *Moral Molecule.*
8. Zak, "Neuroscience of Trust."

9
Activate Empathy

1. Quoted in Goleman, *Social Intelligence,* 29.
2. Quoted in ibid., 58.
3. Quoted in ibid., 59.
4. Szalavitz and Perry, *Born for Love,* 4.
5. Bloom, *Against Empathy.*
6. Ibid., 5.
7. Ibid., 108.
8. Cameron, Inzlicht, and Cunningham, "Empathy Is Actually a Choice."
9. Schumann, Zaki, and Dweck, "Addressing the Empathy Deficit."

10. Sapolsky, *Behave.*

11. De Waal, *Age of Empathy.*

12. Dunbar, *Human Evolution.*

10

Head to the Balcony

1. Heifetz, *Leadership without Easy Answers.*

2. Goleman, *Emotional Intelligence.*

3. Taylor, *My Stroke of Insight,* 18.

4. Panksepp and Biven, *Archaeology of Mind.*

5. Amanda Curtin at the Center for Change in Cambridge, Massachusetts, specializes in treating early childhood trauma and the sensitivity to being retriggered by similar encounters as adults. For more information, see http://www.centerforchange.com.

6. Davidson, *Emotional Life of the Brain.*

7. Ochsner, "How Thinking Controls Feeling."

11

Take Responsibility

1. Samet, *Leadership.*

2. This definition of courage is from www.dictionary.com.

3. Haidt, *Righteous Mind.*

4. Lindner, *Gender, Humiliation, and Global Security.*

5. Hartling and Lindner, "Healing Humiliation."

6. Scheff and Retzinger, *Emotions and Violence.*

12

Advocate for Dignity Education

1. Chaleff, *Courageous Follower.*

2. Weisbord, *Productive Workplaces.*

3. Kegan and Lahey, *An Everyone Culture.*

4. Hartling and Lindner, "Healing Humiliation."

5. Dweck, *Mindset.*

6. Laloux, *Reinventing Organizations.*

7. Kegan and Lahey, *An Everyone Culture*.
8. Samet, *Leadership*.

13
Implement a Dignity Education Program for Everyone

1. For more information about the International Center for Cooperation and Conflict Resolution (ICCCR), see http://icccr.tc.columbia.edu.
2. Iacoboni, *Mirroring People*.

14
Assess Dignity Strengths and Weaknesses

1. Cozolino, *Neuroscience of Psychotherapy*.
2. Ochsner, "How Thinking Controls Feeling."
3. Meeting with Jack Nolan, police commissioner of Dublin, part of the Irish Institute of Boston College program "Alternatives to Political Violence," organized by Bob Mauro, Dublin, January 2013.

15
Address Lingering Wounds to Dignity

1. Hicks, "A Culture of Indignity and Failure of Leadership."
2. Farmer and Gutiérrez, *In the Company of the Poor*.

16
Resolve Current and Future Conflicts with Dignity

1. Kelman, "Informal Mediation."
2. De Waal, *Age of Empathy*.
3. Shapiro, *Negotiating the Nonnegotiable*.
4. Iacoboni, *Mirroring People*.
5. Amnesty International, "Look Refugees in the Eye: Powerful Video Experiment Breaks Down Barriers," May 24, 2016, at https://www.amnesty .org/en/latest/news/2016/05/look-refugees-in-the-eye/.
6. Feinberg, Cheng, and Willer, "Gossip as an Effective and Low-Cost Form of Punishment."

7. Sapolsky, *Behave.*

8. Kahneman, *Thinking Fast and Slow.*

17
The Dignity Pledge

1. Wilson, *Meaning of Human Existence.*

2. Damon and Colby, *Power of Ideals.*

3. Haidt, "New Synthesis in Moral Psychology."

4. Quotation by William Damon and Anne Colby, in Damon and Colby, *Power of Ideals,* 65.

5. Ibid., 57.

6. Chapman and Sisodia, *Everybody Matters,* 121.

18
Normalize Dignity Learning and Practice

1. Dick Cocozza, personal communication, July 2017.

19
Humanity Ascending

1. Fredrickson, *Love 2.0.*

2. Quotation by Gregory L. Fricchione in Fricchione, *Compassion and Healing in Medicine and Society,* 5.

3. Lindner, *Gender, Humiliation, and Global Security.*

4. Szalavitz and Perry, *Born for Love.*

5. Seligman, *Flourish.*

6. I am grateful to Caroline Hayes for introducing me to the idea of "emotional infrastructure."

7. I'd like to thank Dana Born for suggesting that we need to lead not only with dignity, but also for dignity.

Bibliography

Bal, P. Matthijs, and Simon B. de Jong. "From Human Resource Management to Human Dignity Development: A Dignity Perspective on HRM and the Role of Workplace Democracy." Pp. 173–195 in M. Kostera and Michael Pirson, eds., *Dignity and the Organization*. Humanism in Business Series. London: Palgrave MacMillan, 2017.

Barkow, Jerome. *Missing the Revolution: Darwinism for Social Scientists*. Oxford, UK: Oxford University Press, 2006.

Bazerman, Max H. *The Power of Noticing: What the Best Leaders See*. New York: Simon & Schuster, 2014.

Bloom, Paul. *Against Empathy: The Case for Rational Compassion*. New York: HarperCollins, 2016.

Brown, Brené. *Daring Greatly: How the Courage to Be Vulnerable Transforms the Way We Live, Love, Parent, and Lead*. New York: Avery, 2012.

Buss, David. *Evolutionary Psychology: The New Science of the Mind*. Boston: Pearson, Allyn and Bacon, 2004.

Cameron, Daryl, Michael Inzlicht, and William A. Cunningham. "Empathy Is Actually a Choice." *New York Times*, July 10, 2015, http://nyti.ms/1Gc EOYR.

Chaleff, Ira. *The Courageous Follower*. Oakland, CA: Berrett-Koehler, 2009.

Chapman, Bob, and Raj Sisodia. *Everybody Matters: The Extraordinary Power of Caring for Our People Like Family*. New York: Portfolio/Penguin, 2015.

Covey, Stephen M. R., and Douglas R. Conant. "The Connection between Employee Trust and Financial Performance." *Harvard Business Review*, July 16, 2016.

Cozolino, Louis. *The Neuroscience of Psychotherapy*. New York: Norton, 2010.

Damon, William, and Anne Colby. *The Power of Ideals: The Real Story of Moral Choice.* Oxford, UK: Oxford University Press, 2015.

David, Susan. *Emotional Agility: Get Unstuck, Embrace Change, and Thrive in Work and Life.* New York: Avery, 2016.

Davidson, Richard J., with Sharon Begley. *The Emotional Life of Your Brain: How Its Unique Patterns Affect the Way You Think, Feel, and Live—and How You Can Change Them.* New York: Plume, 2013.

de Nalda, Alvaro Lleo, Manuel Guillén, and Ignacio Gil Pechuan. "The Influence of Ability, Benevolence, and Integrity in Trust between Managers and Subordinates: The Role of Ethical Reasoning." *Business Ethics: A European Review* 25, no. 4 (2016): 556–575.

de Waal, Frans. *The Age of Empathy: Nature's Lessons for a Kinder Society.* New York: Harmony Books, 2009.

Dunbar, Robin. *Human Evolution.* Oxford, UK: Oxford University Press, 2016.

Dunbar, Robin I. M., and Louise Barrett. *Handbook of Evolutionary Psychology.* Oxford, UK: Oxford University Press, 2007.

Dweck, Carol S. *Mindset: The New Psychology of Success.* New York: Ballantine, 2006.

Edmondson, Amy C. "Psychological Safety and Learning Behavior in Work Teams." *Administrative Science Quarterly* 44, no. 2 (June 1999): 350–383.

———. *Teaming: How Organizations Learn, Innovate, and Compete in the Knowledge Economy.* San Francisco: Jossey-Bass, 2012.

Eisenberger, N. I., M. D. Lieberman, and K. D. Williams. "Does Rejection Hurt? An fMRI Study of Social Exclusion." *Science* 302, no. 5643 (2003): 290–292.

Farmer, Paul, and Gustavo Gutiérrez. *In the Company of the Poor.* New York: Orbis, 2013.

Feinberg, Matthew, Joey Cheng, and Robb Willer. "Gossip as an Effective and Low-Cost Form of Punishment." *Behavioral and Brain Sciences* 35, no. 1 (February 2012).

Fredrickson, Barbara L. *Love 2.0: Creating Happiness and Health in Moments of Connection.* New York: Plume, 2013.

Fricchione, Gregory L. *Compassion and Healing in Medicine and Society: On the Nature and Use of Attachment Solutions to Separation Challenges.* Baltimore, MD: Johns Hopkins University Press, 2011.

Fuller, Robert. *Somebodies and Nobodies: Overcoming the Abuse of Rank.* Gabriola Island, Canada: New Societies, 2003.

Giles, Sunnie. "The Most Important Leadership Competencies, According to Leaders around the World." *Harvard Business Review,* March 15, 2016.

Goleman, Daniel. *Emotional Intelligence.* New York: Bantam Books, 1995.

———. *Social Intelligence: The New Science of Human Relationships.* New York: Bantam Books, 2006.

Guillén, Manuel, and Tomás F. González. "The Ethical Dimension of Managerial Leadership: Two Illustrative Case Studies in TQM." *Journal of Business Ethics* 34 (2001): 175–189.

Haidt, Jonathan. "The New Synthesis in Moral Psychology." *Science* 316 (2007): 998–1002.

———. *The Righteous Mind: Why Good People Are Divided by Politics and Religion.* New York: Vintage, 2013.

Harari, Yuval Noah. *Sapiens: A Brief History of Humankind.* New York: HarperCollins, 2015.

Hartling, Linda M., and Evelin G. Lindner. "Healing Humiliation: From Reaction to Creative Action." *Journal of Counseling and Development* 94 (2016): 383–390.

Heifetz, Ronald A. *Leadership without Easy Answers.* Cambridge, MA: Harvard University Press, 1998.

Heifetz, Ronald A., and Marty Linsky. *Leadership on the Line: Staying Alive through the Dangers of Leading.* Boston: Harvard Business School Press, 2002.

Hicks, Donna. "A Culture of Indignity and Failure of Leadership." *Humanistic Management Journal* 1, no. 3 (2016): 113–126.

———. *Dignity: Its Essential Role in Resolving Conflict.* New Haven: Yale University Press, 2011.

———. "Dignity Dialogues: An Educational Approach to Healing and Reconciling Relationships in Conflict." In Peter Stearns, ed., *Peacebuilding through Dialogue.* London: Routledge (in press).

Hicks, Donna, and Sandra Waddock. "Dignity, Wisdom, and Tomorrow's Ethical Business Leaders." *Business and Society Review* 121, no. 3 (2015): 447–462.

Hodson, Randy. *Dignity at Work.* Cambridge, UK: Cambridge University Press, 2001.

Iacoboni, Marco. *Mirroring People: The New Science of How We Connect with Others.* New York: Farrar, Straus and Giroux, 2008.

James, William. *The Principles of Psychology.* New York: Henry Holt, 1890.

Kahneman, Daniel. *Thinking Fast and Slow.* New York: Farrar, Straus and Giroux, 2011.

Kegan, Robert, and Lisa Laskow Lahey. *An Everyone Culture: Becoming a Deliberately Developmental Organization.* Boston: Harvard Business Review Press, 2016.

———. *Immunity to Change: How to Overcome It and Unlock the Potential in*

Yourself and Your Organization. Brighton, MA: Harvard Business Review Press, 2009.

Kelman, Herbert C. "Informal Mediation by the Scholar/Practitioner." Pp. 64–96 in J. Bercovitch and J. Z. Rubin, eds., *Mediation in International Relations: Multiple Approaches to Conflict Management.* New York: St. Martin's, 1992.

Laloux, Frederic. *Reinventing Organizations: A Guide to Creating Organizations Inspired by the Next Stage of Human Consciousness.* Brussels: Nelson Parker, 2014.

Lieberman, Matthew D. *Social: Why Our Brains Are Wired to Connect.* New York: Crown, 2013.

Lindner, Evelin. "The Concept of Human Dignity," 2006, www.humiliation studies.org/whoweare/evelin02.php.

———. *Emotion and Conflict.* Westport, CT: Praeger, 2009.

———. *Gender, Humiliation, and Global Security.* Westport, CT: Praeger, 2010.

———. *Making Enemies: Humiliation and International Conflict.* Westport, CT: Praeger Security International, 2006.

Miller, Jean Baker. *Toward a New Psychology of Women.* 2nd ed. Boston: Beacon, 1976.

Mlodinow, Leonard. *Subliminal: How Your Unconscious Mind Rules Your Behavior.* New York: Vintage, 2012.

Ochsner, Kevin. "How Thinking Controls Feeling: A Social Cognitive Neuroscience Approach." Pp. 106–113 in Eddie Harmon-Jones and Piotr Winkielman, eds., *Social Neuroscience.* New York: Guilford, 2007.

Panksepp, Jaak, and Lucy Biven. *The Archaeology of Mind: Neuroevolutionary Origins of Human Emotions.* New York: W. W. Norton, 2012.

Pfeffer, Jeffrey. *Leadership BS: Fixing Workplaces and Careers One Truth at a Time.* New York: HarperCollins, 2015.

Pirson, Michael. *Humanistic Management: Protecting Dignity and Promoting Well-Being.* Cambridge, UK: Cambridge University Press, 2017.

Porath, Christine. *Mastering Civility: A Manifesto for the Workplace.* New York: Grand Central Publishing, 2016.

Robinson, Ken, and Lou Aronica. *Creative Schools: The Grassroots Revolution That's Transforming Education.* New York: Viking, 2015.

Samet, Elizabeth D. *Leadership: Essential Writings by Our Greatest Thinkers.* New York: W. W. Norton, 2015.

Sapolsky, Robert M. *Behave: The Biology of Humans at Our Best and Worst.* New York: Penguin, 2017.

Scheff, Thomas J., and Suzanne M. Retzinger. *Emotions and Violence: Shame and Rage in Destructive Conflicts.* Lexington MA: Lexington Books, 1991.

Schumann, Karine, Jamil Zaki, and Carol S. Dweck. "Addressing the Empathy Deficit: Beliefs about the Malleability of Empathy Predict Effortful Responses When Empathy Is Challenging." *Journal of Personality and Social Psychology* 107 (2014): 475–493.

Seligman, Martin E. P. *Flourish: A Visionary New Understanding of Happiness and Well-Being.* New York: Atria, 2012.

Shapiro, Daniel. *Negotiating the Nonnegotiable: How to Resolve Your Most Emotionally Charged Conflicts.* New York: Viking, 2016.

Stone, Douglas, and Sheila Heen. *Thanks for the Feedback: The Science and Art of Receiving Feedback Well.* New York: Penguin, 2014.

Szalavitz, Maia, and Bruce D. Perry. *Born for Love: Why Empathy Is Essential and Endangered.* New York: Harper, 2010.

Tannenbaum, Melanie. "'But I Didn't Mean It.' Why It's So Hard to Prioritize Impacts over Intents." *Scientific American Blog Network,* October 14, 2014.

Taylor, Jill Bolte. *My Stroke of Insight: A Brain Scientist's Personal Journey.* New York: Viking, 2006.

Thoreau, Henry David. *Civil Disobedience and Other Essays.* Mineola, NY: Dover Thrift Editions, 1993.

Valcour, Monique. "The Power of Dignity in the Workplace." *Harvard Business Review,* April 28, 2014.

von Kimakowitz, Ernst, et al. "Introducing This Book and Humanistic Management." Pp. 1–12 in Ernst von Kimakowitz et al., *Humanistic Management Practice.* Humanism in Business Series. London: Palgrave Macmillan, 2010.

Weisbord, Marvin R. *Productive Workplaces: Dignity, Meaning, and Community in the Twenty-First Century.* San Francisco: Jossey Bass, 2012.

Wilson, Edward O. *The Meaning of Human Existence.* New York: Liveright, 2014.

———. *Social Conquest of the Earth.* New York: Liveright, 2012.

Zak, Paul J. *The Moral Molecule: The Source of Love and Prosperity.* New York: Dutton, 2012.

———. "The Neuroscience of Trust." *Harvard Business Review* (January–February 2017 online issue); https://hbr.org/2017/01/the-neuroscience-of-trust.

Index

Reader's Guide

1. Dr. Hicks, how do you define dignity? Is it the same thing as respect?

Dignity is not the same as respect. This is the most common misconception that I encounter when introducing the concept to people and organizations. Dignity is something we are born with—it is our inherent value and worth. We have little trouble seeing it when a child is born; there is no question about whether she or he is something of value. In fact, we would say that infants are *invaluable, priceless,* and *irreplaceable.* How do we treat something that is invaluable, priceless, and irreplaceable? We give it our utmost care and attention. Even though we are all born worthy of this care and attention, we are born vulnerable to having our dignity violated. Treating others with dignity, then, becomes the baseline of our interactions. You don't have to do anything to deserve dignity. Respect, on the other hand, needs to be earned. If I say I respect someone, that person has done something remarkable to earn my respect. I feel admiration for her. She is a role model for how I want to be in the world.

2. What is dignity consciousness, and why is it important?

People have no idea how much dignity dominates our desire to be treated well and to be in relationships that make us feel safe, seen, heard, and valued. When we learn how to honor dignity, it creates strong, healthy relationships and an enduring sense of well-being. *Dignity consciousness* gives us the internal, emotional scaffolding that enables us to live our lives in full extension and to contribute to the well-being of everyone around us.

3. Your background is in international conflict management and diplomacy. What do international conflicts have to do with what happens in the workplace?

When we human beings are mistreated, when our dignity has been violated, we are hardwired to react to threats to our well-being. Our self-preservation instincts are triggered, and we want revenge, to get even with those who have violated us. This human reaction happens whenever we feel threatened by others, no matter where we are. It happens in intimate relationships, families, workplaces, and in the international arena. We have a hard time letting go of assaults to our dignity.

4. Why is honoring dignity so important, especially for people in leadership positions?

Leaders play a crucial role in creating a culture that brings out the best in people. They need to know how to honor the dignity of their people as well as create policies that are sensitive to dignity issues. The leadership team needs to be on board with dignity awareness if it is to become a way of life at work, both by modeling dignified behaviors and by creating a culture that is mindful of the effect they have on all employees.

5. Honoring someone's dignity seems like it should be so simple to do. Aren't these leaders who don't just bad people who don't care about their employees?

Honoring dignity is not so simple. We may all be born with dignity, but we are not born knowing how to act like it. That has to be learned. My experience is that this lack of dignity consciousness just means that people have not learned how to treat one another in a way that demonstrates value and appreciation. Most of the leaders I have worked with are good people with good intentions who have had no education in how to be in healthy, affirming relationships built on an understanding of dignity.

6. What is the most common way leaders violate people's dignity at work?

When I do an assessment of the ways employees feel their dignity is violated in their workplaces, the most common response, no matter where I am, is a violation of their sense of safety (one of the Ten Elements of Dignity). It is not that they don't feel physically safe—they do not feel psychologically safe to speak up when something bad happens at work. They are terrified of speaking up about ways in which their managers and leaders have violated their dignity. The fear is that if they do speak up, they might receive a bad performance review, and in extreme cases, perhaps lose their jobs.

7. We often talk about "toxic workplaces" and how to fix them. What's the role of dignity in these situations?

A toxic workplace is one whose culture implicitly (and sometimes explicitly) condones dignity-violating behaviors. The unspoken norms enable hurtful interactions between management and employees and between employees. These are work-

places where the effects of dignity violations are not understood and have become normalized. Ignorance of all things
related to dignity overtakes the culture, creating wounded and
unhappy employees.

8. What are the signs that a workplace culture has a dignity problem?

Two things: conflicts and gossip. My experience has shown
that most conflicts in the workplace have underlying, unaddressed violations of dignity at their core. A robust gossip network also demonstrates that people do not feel safe to speak
up when something bad happens to them and the negative
effects of those violations go straight to the gossip mill. Matt
Feinberg and his colleagues write: "Gossip represents a widespread, efficient and low-cost form of punishment."[1] If you are
too afraid to confront the person who violated you, gossip is
one way of seeking revenge and getting even.

9. When it comes to resolving conflict, you argue we don't need common ground; we need "higher ground." What does that mean?

When people engage in dignity-violating behaviors that are at
the core of conflicts, they are driven by base, self-preservation
instincts that bring out the worst of what they are capable of.
We can do so much better than that. What we need is to ele-
vate the interactions with an understanding of dignity—that
which we all yearn for and is our highest common denominator. The way to this higher ground is dignity consciousness.

---

1. Matthew Feinberg, Joey T. Cheng, and Robb Willer, "Gossip as an Effective and Low-Cost Form of Punishment," *Behavorial and Brain Sciences*
35, no. 1 (February 2012): 25.

10. One of the key components of leading with dignity is taking responsibility. Why is this important?

This goes back to the hardwired self-preservation instincts that we are all born with. (I have named them the Ten Temptations to Violate Dignity.) When we make a mistake, these self-preservation instincts do not want us to take responsibility for it. Looking bad in the eyes of others is something we avoid like the plague. Instead, our instincts want us to cover up, lie, and blame and shame others instead of coming clean. Dignity consciousness allows us to override these base instincts, take responsibility for our actions, and, in so doing, maintain our dignity.

11. It is important for leaders to learn how to be good at treating everyone with dignity, but they are also responsible for making sure that the policies they create are dignity honoring. Explain.

If a leader wants to create a culture of dignity, it is important not only to have interpersonal skills in honoring dignity but also to be mindful of the importance of developing policies that honor dignity. Those who impose system-wide decisions that are implemented from the top need to be mindful of the effects of their decisions on all of their employees. For example, if a policy is created that favors one group over others or discriminates against some groups, that policy will encourage resentment within the system, contributing to a toxic work culture.

12. What is the one thing you hope leaders will take away from this book?

I would like them to think about how much time and effort they have committed to their professional education—advanced degrees and work experience that have gotten them to where they are. If they were to dedicate a fraction of that time to educating themselves about dignity, they would improve their capacity to become not just a good leader but a great leader.